Pas de Deux

Florida A&M University
Florida Atlantic University
Florida Gulf Coast University
Florida International University
Florida State University
New College of Florida
University of Central Florida
University of Florida
University of North Florida
University of South Florida
University of West Florida

University Press of Florida

Gainesville · Tallahassee · Tampa · Boca Raton · Pensacola · Orlando · Miami · Jacksonville · Ft. Myers · Sarasota

Pas de Deux

A Textbook on Partnering

SECOND EDITION

By Nikolai Nikolaevich Serebrennikov

Edited by Marian Horosko

Translated by Elizabeth Kraft with added second edition material translated by Sergey Gordeev

Cover photo by Rosalie O'Connor

Library of Congress Cataloging-in-Publication Data

Serebrennikov, Nikolai Nikolaevich.
[Podderzhka v duetnom tantse. English]
Pas de deux: a textbook on partnering / by Nikolai
Nikolaevich Serebrennikov; edited by Marian Horosko;
translated by Elizabeth Kraft.—2nd ed. / with added
second edition material translated by Sergey Gordeev.
      p. cm.
ISBN 978-0-8130-1768-6 (paper: alk. paper)
1. Pas de deux. I. Horosko, Marian. II. Title.
GV1788.2.P37S49 2000
792.8'2—dc21 00-027619

The University Press of Florida is the scholarly publishing
agency for the State University System of Florida,
comprising Florida A&M University, Florida Atlantic
University, Florida Gulf Coast University, Florida
International University, Florida State University, New
College of Florida, University of Central Florida,
University of Florida, University of North Florida,
University of South Florida, and University of West
Florida.

University Press of Florida
15 Northwest 15th Street
Gainesville, FL 32611
www.upf.com

Contents

Sketches

Preface

PAS DE DEUX is one of the leading disciplines in the curriculum of the Vaganova Ballet Academy and deserves scrupulous attention. The transition from a nine-year to an eight-year program at the academy had a grave effect on this discipline because fifteen- or sixteen-year-old young men are not yet ready for great physical exertion, and young women of that age have already fully matured, and, as a rule, exceed young men in physical weight.

The general physical exertion of dance students is considerable, and they must be given constant medical attention. Female students who need to lose extra weight must receive professional medical guidance rather than amateur treatment at home.

In teaching the art of ballet, much attention is given to developing the muscles of the torso and legs and a negligible amount of time to developing the shoulder muscles. This oversight primarily affects young men as they learn to lift in their pas de deux classes. For several years at the Vaganova Academy, experiments in special classes with boys from the fifth and sixth grades (fourteen to sixteen years of age) have included training the muscles of the arms, back, and abdominals, as well as developing quickness of reaction, dexterity, and the ability to sense a partner's balance. Those experiments showed positive results, and such training should be encouraged everywhere.

Students have different abilities. Some, for example, have mediocre ability in classical dance but show excellence in folk dance. Others may be clearly gifted in acting, while others, with incredible accuracy, respond to a style and an era of historical dance. These are the tendencies that determine the specialty of the future ballet artist.

Students also differ in their ability to perform pas de deux with lifts. Some women struggle with their difference in height and weight from partners who may lack physical strength or height. Other women struggle because they cannot sense their own bodies in the air, and both partners may be unable to develop a mutual feeling of rhythm. Young women must also develop a good jump, strong shoulder and arm muscles, and especially strong and flexible upper back muscles. Therefore, in order to fairly evaluate a student's progress in duet dance, three grades should be given at the end of each semester: one for professional suitability to the subject; another for diligence and productivity; and the third for actual accomplishment—the same evaluation as used for grading classical technique. At the same time, such a multi-dimensional evaluation will give teachers insight into a student's character.

Much is required of today's teachers. They must continually increase their mastery of pedagogy, perfect their teaching methodologies, and enrich their knowledge of related disciplines. It is important to attend the classes of other teachers and to analyze their methods. Teachers should actively participate in meetings on methods and join committees with other teachers of pas de deux, where specific questions relating to the responsibility of teaching the younger generation are discussed.

In Russia, national seminars are of great methodological help. There, teachers discuss the main problems involved in teaching the subject, determine the directions in which the method should develop, and give qualified answers to many questions which arise in everyday practice. Each seminar is prepared in advance and has several rehearsals, which inevitably results in a concert-like quality with a showing of the result of a certain period of work. This is always interesting, useful, and necessary. No less interesting and useful for the teacher is to see the drafting process of another teacher's work, to see the mistakes of the students, and to watch how a teacher corrects those mistakes and gets the desired results. This results in the teacher's increased ability to understand the methodology of teaching theoretically as well as practically by actually seeing it. This is the most effective way towards perfection for the teacher.

Teachers should be given more opportunities to go on trips to different dance schools within a country. Such interaction would definitely give positive results in the strengthening of theoretical knowledge and in the mutual enriching and broadening of a teacher's horizons, as well as provide more precisely determined goals in the aesthetic training of students.

ALTHOUGH THERE ARE many good textbooks, there is a need for visual methodological aids such as captioned photo albums and academic films or videos with accompanying text. Each school should have a film library which would serve as a useful aid, not only for the students, but for teachers as well. At year-end exams for each subject, there are always one or two exercises or combinations which, because of their artistic and academic qualities, can serve as examples. It is essential to record these exercises on film or video tape.

All special disciplines, because they enhance one another, are equally important for the harmonious development of a modern ballet artist. For that reason, all graduation exams should be accepted by a federal qualifications committee which will help students correctly understand and realize the multi-dimensionality of their profession.

One of the most important goals of the dance school is to maintain a constant, creative connection to a theater that develops its activities in two directions: the preservation of masterpieces of classical ballet heritage and the creation of new works that are diverse in form and deep in content. These two directions are the determining ones in teaching the art of choreography. The choice of works from the heritage for academic purposes must be made with consideration of each student's ability and capability. A bad choice will only do harm. Although certain technical elements of pas de deux must necessarily be included in the curriculum, these must not exceed the range of the class. No less strict a judgment should be applied in the choice of work from modern choreography. Before all else, the teacher must make sure that the chosen work has artistic value and, only then, evaluate its academic usefulness.

In pas de deux classes, our students master the technique of partnering and lifts, learn a series of duets and, at the same time, do exercises to learn communicating from the stage. We call this a "compulsory program" that must be completed by every student in order to receive a diploma. Students with more talent and potential are given additional training in duet dance with pas de deux of considerable technical difficulty and artistic challenge. Such classes for second- and third-year students should be conducted once a week on an extracurricular basis during rehearsal periods. Beyond a doubt, such classes increase the professionalism of gifted students, promote creative growth in the theater, and bring about perfect duets.

This textbook only lays a foundation for ongoing discussions about pas de deux dance that will hopefully generate new books and articles on the history of duet dance, its methodologies and teaching perspectives, and an evolving aesthetics of pas de deux choreography.

Nikolai Serebrennikov

Introduction

SEREBRENNIKOV'S textbook on pas de deux dance fulfills a long-standing need in the training of American dancers for a comprehensive system in the study of partnering. His system can be adapted successfully to lifts incorporated into ice dancing, ballroom dance, or dancesport.

Serebrennikov had performed with the Kirov Ballet and was teaching at the Vaganova Ballet Academy (formerly the Leningrad Choreographic Institute) in St. Petersburg when the first edition of his book was released in 1969. When I met him in 1994 at the Academy, he gave me his latest edition (1985) and admonished me to be meticulous in the translation of his revised book as I had promised him when my first limited edition appeared in 1979.

In this second edition, Serebrennikov has added more sketches of poses, his advice on teaching, which appears in the preface, and photographs of Russian ballet stars. The last two chapters describe suitable lifts and poses for theatrical ballroom dance or exhibition dancing. The ballet terms derive from the Vaganova method, but are easily understood by teachers following the Cecchetti and Royal Academy of Dancing (R.A.D.) systems.

SEREBRENNIKOV'S format describes a principle by tracing its easiest to its most difficult execution in the same chapter. For this reason, it is advisable to construct the early classes by giving the easier exercises and progressing to the more advanced as the students master the material. In a well-structured class, for example, the teacher might choose a promenade or balance, a tour, and a lift based upon the mastery level of the group rather than trying to teach chapter by chapter.

Some Facts to Remember

The current Russian floor plan defines the corners of a space, classroom, or stage by dividing it into eight numbered directions. At point 1, the performer is centered in the space and faces the audience or mirror; point 3 is a one-quarter turn to the right; point 5 is a half turn directly back; and point 7 is a three-quarter turn. The corners of the room are numbered 2, 4, 6, and 8. (See sketch 1.) Therefore, turning to the right, the eight divisions are: point 1 (audience), corner 2, point 3, corner 4, point 5, corner 6, point 7, and corner 8.

Although Russian terminology is used throughout the text, occasional references to other methodologies may be beneficial:

POSITIONS OF THE ARMS

RUSSIAN	CECCHETTI	R.A.D.
Preparatory	5th en bas	bras bas
1st	5th en avant	1st
2nd	2nd	2nd
3rd	5th en haut	5th

POSITIONS OF THE FEET

In the study of pas de deux, as in ballet and modern dance choreography, the boy and girl sometimes use Sixth Position—feet together as in First, but not turned out, with the feet almost parallel and both knees facing front.

Retiré describes the pose in which the working thigh is raised to the Second Position en l'air with the knee bent so that the pointed toe rests in front of, behind, or to the side of the supporting knee.

Passé is used when the working leg is bent and brought back to the supporting leg before passing through and stretching outward into another pose such as développé. Throughout the text, the positions of the feet and arms are capitalized to avoid confusion. Refer to the sketches.

Rhythm

The boy and girl must react to each other rhythmically by coordinating their movements through correct breathing. Generally speaking, there is a small exhale through the mouth during a plié and a larger inhale that expands the rib cage outward during a lift or turn. Classroom rules for breathing should be strictly maintained, and in no instance should the breath be held more than a few seconds. During a lift, the boy's hands should be placed below the girl's rib cage and must never press her ribs.

Tempo

Both partners must know the exact counts of every movement and should respond to the beat of the music at the same time, in the same way. This general rule applies to all movements, especially for lifts and jumps to be in harmony.

The boy must learn to feel or sense the girl's balance in all movements, especially in multiple tours, and must hold her firmly at the end of the turns. A firm hold is required in promenades and in any lift. In all cases, the girl initiates the movement; the boy completes it.

The boy, in pas de deux dance, does not use his full turnout but keeps a broad base, approximating First, Second, Fourth, and Fifth Positions as described in the text and as illustrated in the sketches. He must keep the girl's weight centered at all times.

Technique

The principles of good technique apply in pas de deux dance. The teacher must be watchful that the partners maintain the center line of balance throughout. The girl's arms must not overly cross especially before a lift, nor be held too far back. The movements must be clearly understood by both partners. From the beginning, the teacher should make sure that both partners maintain their central line of balance in the épaulement positions. The girl must learn to execute a position and hold it until both she and her partner have completed the movement or lift.

With young dancers or beginners in pas de deux at any age, it is important for the teacher to keep the students calm, patient, secure in the knowledge that the Russian methodology is to be trusted over personal theories.

Until they develop confidence, it is wise to have a "spotter," another student, nearby whenever a new lift is attempted or when students practice without the teacher present. Should a lift be improperly executed, the spotter must be especially mindful that the girl's head NEVER hit the floor. Tutus may be worn during the class and serve the useful purpose of accustoming the boy to sensing his distance from his partner as well as her center of balance.

The class structure may include two lines of alternately positioned boys and girls. The girls execute a movement, then move to the right to the next partner. At the end of the line, the girl moves to the second line, executing the movement to the left. The lines exchange places as they do in regular technique classes. The combinations may be done on the diagonal or in a circle as well. A simple, classical pas de deux—such as the Ballade, or "Wheat" from Act I of *Coppélia*—may become the goal of the first year.

The rewards of following Serebrennikov's pedagogy are plentiful. The teacher will not only find that each student's solo technique has been enhanced and redefined through mastery of the material, but that such results have been achieved in the safe, correct, and beautiful execution of the art of partnering.

Marian Horosko

Pas de Deux

1 · Finding the Point of Balance

FINDING the point of balance is the first principle to be mastered. Basic support methods for the boys are: his placing two hands on the girl's waist; his two hands holding both of the girl's hands; his one hand holding only one of her hands; and his one hand at her waist. In addition, a combination of these methods is used in static or en place poses, in changes from pose to pose, in turns, promenades, falls, ports de bras and in returning to the starting pose.

Finding the Point of Balance during Small Movements with Two Hands Supporting at the Waist

When supporting the girl at the waist, the boy stands in a modified Second Position, slightly turned out, directly behind the girl regardless of the spectator's view. In facing any corner or point of the eight divisions of the room or stage (Sketch 1), he must still stand directly behind her. His hands are along her beltline, wrists held downwards, the palm and the four fingers of each hand held firmly on the sides of the girl's body at waist level, little fingers resting above the hip and thumbs stretched slightly upwards pressing firmly on the girl's large spinal muscles.

The girl does a demi-plié in Fifth Position, then relevés into Fifth Position sur les pointes. (Sketch 2. Relevé sur les pointes, front and

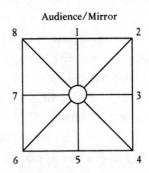

1. Divisions of the stage
Russian system: corners are
2, 4, 6, 8; points are 1, 3, 5, 7

side views.) From the first lesson in pas de deux, the girl must never be allowed to displace a hip or hop on pointe when attempting to balance. The boy must not allow his partner to find her balance independently as it interferes with his understanding of the principles of partnering. To check the girl's balance, her partner may remove his hands for an instant in the final pose sur les pointes. If she keeps her balance and remains upright, she has been properly placed and is retaining her correct alignment.

2. Relevé sur les pointes, front and side views

Finding the Point of Balance in Sur le Cou-de-Pied

From Fifth Position, the girl does a demi-plié and relevés into sur le cou-de-pied devant sur la pointe, pointed position. The boy holds the girl at the waist with both hands and finds her center of balance. (Sketch 3. Finding the point of balance in sur le cou-de-pied.) The boy must shift her center of balance from two feet in demi-plié to the center of her supporting leg. The girl then lowers softly through the supporting foot before closing the lifted foot into Fifth Position. (Sketch 4. Descending through the foot from pointe through half-pointe to demi-plié before closing the lifted foot into Fifth Position.) Repeat the exercise lifting the back foot into sur le cou-de-pied derrière; and from demi-plié in Second and Fourth Positions, descending through the supporting foot before placing the working foot into the starting position. The shift of weight is from a broad base of two legs to a narrower base onto one leg. Throughout the exercises a slow and strict tempo should be kept.

There are a number of binding or connecting steps, such as pas de bourrée, glissade, pas couru, flic-flac, pas chassé, and pas marchés, which should be practiced with and without a change of feet and mastered with the boy standing directly behind or at the side of the girl, two hands on her waist, before combining these movements in an enchaînement.

3. Finding the point of balance in sur le cou-de-pied

4. Descending through the foot from pointe through half-pointe to demi-plié before closing the lifted foot into Fifth Position

Finding the Point of Balance in Pas de Bourrée without Changing Feet

The boy shifts with the girl's center of gravity from one foot to the other while repeating her movements himself in a modified turnout. In lowering her from pointe, he shifts her weight onto the whole foot. The boy should transfer the weight of the girl's body from one hand to the other when she repeats the movements to the opposite side.

Finding the Point of Balance in Pas de Bourrée Changing Feet

The method is the same as above, but the boy turns the girl slightly at the waist so that she finishes in the correct épaulement position.

Finding the Point of Balance in Pas de Bourrée en Tournant

The boy moves his hands along the girl's beltline in the direction OPPOSITE to the direction of the turn. He then gives a light push forward with the hand that was drawn back and a pull backwards with the hand that was placed forward. This push-pull signal to turn is given by applying hand pressure at the girl's waist. The boy's hands follow along the beltline in the DIRECTION OF THE TURN as she turns until he stops her at the end in a given pose by squeezing her waist with his hands to stop the momentum of the turn. This kind of hand signal frequently precedes movements and is part of what Serebrennikov calls the "common tempo" in pas de deux partnering. It is almost imperceptible when correctly performed.

Finding the Point of Balance in Pas Couru and Pas Chassé

These movements should be practiced in different directions and in a circle, the boy moving simultaneously with the girl in a simplified form (less exactly or perfectly than he would alone), in a walking step or repeated chassés, at a strict tempo and at a consistent distance, usually about twelve inches away to allow for the width of the tutu.

Finding the Point of Balance in Pas Balancé and Pas Glissade

Practice these movements with and without change of feet and with the girl going around the boy. He may turn around himself or stand still. If he turns around himself en place, he supports the girl the entire time as she circles him. If he stands still, he must be ready to support her in the final given pose after she finishes her circle around him. The boy must not move as it is up to the girl to calculate the pas glissade or pas balancé so that it is a comfortable distance for his support.

At a later time, if the glissade is a preparation for a jump, the boy should hold one side of the girl's waist and move with her so that, at the moment of the jump, he is very slightly behind and ahead of her on one side and can guide her with the slight impetus he gives from that hand as he grasps her waist with the other hand.

Finding the Point of Balance during Big Movements with Two Hands Supporting at the Waist

In support of développé, grand rond de jambe, retiré, grand ports de bras at 45 or 90 degrees, the boy moves the girl's point of balance onto the supporting leg and returns the trunk or hips to the center of balance during the lowering of the leg to the starting position.

Finding the Point of Balance in Développé

In développé devant at 90 degrees. (Sketch 5. Développé devant at 90 degrees, inclination from the perpendicular.) The girl is in Fifth Position de face, right devant. The boy is behind her, hands on her waist, as both make a slight demi-plié. She relevés into Fifth Position. While she is still on both feet, the boy moves her weight slightly onto her left pointe and towards himself. When she feels she is on her left pointe, she begins the développé devant. She must not be permitted to sink into her supporting leg or to twist her working leg. The boy firmly holds her weight until the end of her movement, and when she lowers her leg to Fifth Position sur les pointes, he transfers her weight slightly forwards onto her own feet. Both should finish in a slight demi-plié as she descends onto her heels.

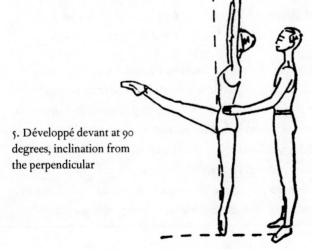

5. Développé devant at 90 degrees, inclination from the perpendicular

Finding the Point of Balance in Grand Port de Bras Penchée

The girl stands in First Arabesque on the right foot sur la pointe. The boy stands behind the girl on the right foot, left in pointe tendue derrière without too much turnout, with the stretched leg resting on the ball of the foot for a more stable position. His left hand can be seen from the front around her back, with his right hand on the right side of her body next to him. The girl does a grand port de bras devant (penchée), a bend directly forwards from the waist as she moves her arms into preparatory position and recovers her arabesque line with the body upwards again. (In grand port de bras the girl may bend or circle her body at or just under shoulder level, or bend or circle her body from the waist.) The boy shifts her center of gravity slightly forward and holds this support until she bends upwards and returns to the starting arabesque position when he again shifts her weight onto the right leg. The arabesque may be a First, Second, Third, or Fourth Arabesque. (Sketch 6. First, Second, Third, and Fourth Arabesques, Russian method. Note position of boy's hands and his stance.)

Big poses can be studied from en place position or with different approaches. The boy can be standing behind the girl with both hands at the waist, next to her, or facing her.

Finding the Point of Balance in Small and Large Poses with Two Hands at the Waist from En Place Positions or Different Approaches

These should be studied at first en place and then with various steps into a pose. These exercises should be a combination where the boy stands en place and girl takes one step towards him, where both take one step towards each other, or where the boy moves toward the girl. The movement towards the partner can be made with or without a hold. It is important that the boy anticipate the moment when he must center the girl's weight.

If the boy stands en place, the girl must concentrate on the size of her step towards him and must move straight into a pose with her legs absolutely con-

6. First, Second, Third, and Fourth Arabesques, Russian method

trolled and her spine firmly held. The boy's pose or position must harmonize with that of the girl, and he must always remember not to use full turnout and to keep his own weight firmly over the three points of balance of the foot (big and small toes and heel). Temps lié at 90 degrees is the most useful exercise since it uses a step from demi-plié into a pose. (Sketch 7. Attitude effacée and attitude croisée with a two-hand hold.) (Sketch 8. Pose écartée devant and derrière with a two-hand hold.) (Sketch 9. Pose croisée devant and effacée devant with a two-hand hold.)

7. Attitude effacée
and attitude croisée
with a two-hand
hold

ATTITUDE EFFACÉE   ATTITUDE CROISÉE

8. Pose écartée
devant and derrière
with a two-hand
hold

ÉCARTÉ TO CORNER 2   ÉCARTÉ TO CORNER 4

9. Pose croisée
devant and
effacée devant
with a two-
hand hold

DÉVELOPPÉ CROISÉ   DÉVELOPPÉ EFFACÉ

2 · Finding the Point of Balance for Incomplete Turns

SEREBRENNIKOV categorizes turns in two forms: the "complete" turn of 360 degrees and the "incomplete" turn that is 3/4, 1/2, or 1/4 of a complete turn. There are four definitions for a turn in the Russian system: TURN means the boy turns the girl without giving impetus; PROMENADE means the boy turns the girl by walking around her; REVOLVE means the boy and girl turn around each other forwards, backwards, or dos-à-dos; PIROUETTE means the girl takes "force"—as in executing the turn alone—as her partner holds his hands in the appropriate position away from but encircling her waist. Later, he must learn how to give "impetus" to increase the number of her turns.

Maintaining Balance During an Incomplete Turn

The first exercise should begin with the boy standing behind the girl who is sur les pointes. The boy places both hands on the girl's waist and, using equal pressure on each side of her waist, he directs one hand forwards and the other backwards. If the turn is to the right, the boy's right hand slides from the right side of the waist along the beltline forward almost to the front of her waist. At the same time, his left hand slides along the beltline toward the center of her back. He then exerts a light pressure as a signal to begin the turn. Moving the hands slightly left before a turn to the right gives impetus to the movement from a static position. The turn may be a 1/4, 1/2, 3/4, or full turn. The boy must determine how much "push" to give on the supporting side depending upon the number of turns required. He must learn to control the movement of his hands so that the girl's turn is always smooth.

The preparation for an incomplete or complete turn may begin from demi-plié during which the boy places his hands along the girl's beltline OPPOSITE to the direction of the turn. (Sketch 10. Preparatory position before pirouette en dedans.) Before the girl's relevé into the pose of the turn—her left foot will be in retiré—he gives a slight signal for the turn to the RIGHT to begin. He keeps his hands moving along her waist during the turn, now in the direction of the turn as it progresses, and stops her in a given pose. If the exercises to find the center of the girl's balance in the previous chapter have not been mastered, the turns will not be smooth.

10. Preparatory position before pirouette en dedans

Maintaining Balance in a Slow Incomplete Turn Ending in Attitude Croisée

The girl faces front and stands on her left pointe with the right leg à la seconde at 90 degrees. The boy stands behind her, hands on her waist, and moves his right hand towards her back and his left hand forward to the front of the waist (Sketch 11a). After a light signal, he slowly turns her to the LEFT as she places her right foot into retiré position. At the same time, she raises her arms into Third Position (Sketch 11b). When she has been turned slowly and faces corner 2, she finishes the movement in attitude croisée derrière as the boy takes a small step or lunge in the direction of corner 2 behind her (Sketch 11c).

At this level, the teacher may give a wide assortment of movements as finishing poses, incorporating those mastered in Chapter One: attitude effacée; écartés to corners 2 and 8; developpé effacé; and First, Second, Third and Fourth Arabesques with 1/2, 1/4, or 3/4 incomplete turns on both the right and left sides.

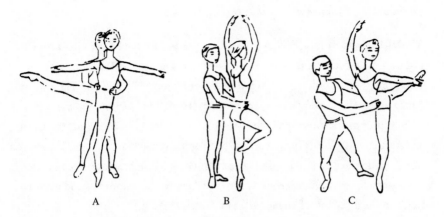

A   B   C

11a, 11b, 11c. Turns from à la seconde at 90 degrees into attitude croisée

Maintaining Balance in a Slow Incomplete Turn with the Girl Approaching the Boy

The girl stands in en face or facing point 1, in Fifth Position, right foot front. The boy stands to her right at a distance of about one large step. The girl takes one step to the right into demi-plié on the right foot and relevés onto pointe with a half turn; she ends facing the boy as he quickly places his hands on her waist and holds her in balance. She développés her left leg à la seconde at 90 degrees raising her arms into Third Position.

(Sketch 12. À la seconde at 90 degrees facing the partner.) From there, he slides his hands in the direction OPPOSITE to her turn as she, slowing, performs an incomplete turn ending in any given pose.

12. À la seconde at 90 degrees facing the partner

Maintaining Balance in a Quick Incomplete Turn

The girl stands en face, facing point 1, on the left foot sur la pointe with the right leg raised à la seconde at 90 degrees, arms in Second Position. The boy stands behind her holding her waist with both hands. He shifts his right hand backwards, left hand forwards, and with a SHARP movement gives a signal, giving force or impetus for a turn to the LEFT, en dedans. During the turn, the girl's arms move into Third Position, but the leg remains in à la seconde position at 90 degrees until her right leg and right shoulder reach corner 6. She then turns herself into attitude croisée derrière where the boy stops her and makes a lunge in the direction of corner 2 (as in Sketch 11c).

This exercise, similar to the first slow series which also began in an à la seconde position, requires both more force to swing the leg 1/2 a turn while keeping it in the extended position of 90 degrees as well as a sharp twist to the left by the girl to change into attitude croisée derrière.

Serebrennikov adds: "In all forms of grand fouetté en tournant, en dehors, and en dedans with or without demi-plié before rising onto pointe, the boy uses the same method of support in the incomplete turn. Turns may be studied in the following positions: with the partners side by side, face to face, boy and girl facing point 1, boy on one or both knees. In studying turns, it is recommended not to overload the combinations with complicated positions and to take into consideration the degree of mastery that can be achieved by the class."

Maintaining Balance in a Tour Lent (Promenade), *a Slow 360 Degree Turn in a Given Pose*

Tour lent is a slow turn where the girl, who is standing on one leg sur la pointe, is led by the boy, who is holding her by the wrist or by the hand as he walks in a circle around her. Small poses (such as sur le cou-de-pied) or big poses (such as attitude effacée) may be used in a promenade. The toe of the girl's supporting foot serves as the pivotal center of the circle.

After the girl has taken her position, the boy, in a turn that goes to the RIGHT, takes the first step of the circle on his LEFT foot, then puts the right foot to the toe of the left foot, and continues to walk in this heel-to-toe manner in a circle. In turning to the left, he takes the first step with the RIGHT or outside foot. He must not shuffle his feet nor mince his steps. It is important that the boy not change the circumference of the circle as he walks around the girl in an easy manner without tension. The girl should assist the turn by pushing forward with the heel of her supporting foot. It is vital that the girl maintain her pose strongly throughout the promenade. When the partners promenade en face, the elbows of the supporting arms of BOTH the boy and girl should be maintained in a correct First Position throughout the promenade. (This position is sometimes called an "S" curve because both partners keep the elbows raised in First Position.)

At first, according to Serebrennikov, promenades should be done in a slow tempo without changing the starting pose. Later, the poses may be changed through passé, grand rond de jambe, and other more complex movements. As the boy moves in the circle, he may walk at the side of the girl or face her, moving backwards or forwards.

3 · Finding the Point of Balance for Complete Turns

SEREBRENNIKOV points out that the girl's arms play an important part in the correct execution of complete or multiple turns. He describes the three arm positions as:

1. a shortened First Position in which one arm quickly joins the other already curved across the chest during the preparation, with the elbows away from the sides of her body so that the boy's hands are not impeded. The level of her hands should be four to five inches away from the level of her rib cage (Sketch 13a).
2. both arms raised directly into Third Position above the head with no lean forward or backward, so that one could draw an imaginary straight line through the center of the figure (Sketch 13b).
3. crossed at the chest level and tightly pressed to the body so as not to touch the partner. (Sketch 13a, 13b, 13c. Positions of the girl's arms in tours.)

Serebrennikov defines the problems in finding the point of balance in turns for the boy: learning to shift the girl's center of gravity to help her find the correct and comfortable preparation for taking force; maintaining the girl's balance during the turn and preserving the vertical axis of her turn by returning her to the correct position should she lean; stopping the girl exactly in the given pose sharply or smoothly depending upon the given tempo without foreshortening the pose from the audience's point of view.

13a, 13b, 13c. Position of
the girl's arms in tours

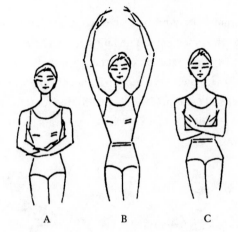

A   B   C

Preparation for a Turn En Dehors from Fourth Position
without the Turn

The girl stands in Fifth Position, right foot devant, arms in Preparatory Position. The boy stands behind her in Second Position with both hands on her waist. (Sketch 14. Position of the boy's hands on the girl's waist at the start and end of a turn.) She does a demi-plié and a relevé onto pointe of the left foot with the right in sur le cou-de-pied position devant, arms raised to First Position. During this move, the boy shifts her center of gravity slightly forward and onto the left foot as he moves his right foot backwards into a modified Fourth Position.

The girl then takes a Fourth Position, right foot back; her right arm remains in First Position, the left in Second, or both arms are held in Second, palms facing the floor. (Sketch 15a. Boy and girl in Fourth Position preparations.) The girl then does a relevé onto the left pointe, right foot sur le cou-de-pied devant

14. Position of the boy's hands on
the girl's waist at the start and end
of a turn

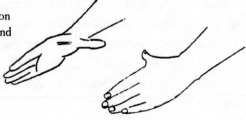

while immediately bringing her left arm sharply into First and omitting the turn for the time being. The boy slightly changes the girl's center of balance from the Fourth Position onto the left foot, leaving her hips slightly forward, and draws his own right foot up from Fourth Position to stand erect in a modified Second Position. (Sketch 15b. Position for the turn with the boy in modified Second Position.) The exercise ends in a small or large pose given by the teacher.

15a. Boy and girl in Fourth Position preparations

15b. Position for the turn with the boy in modified Second Position

Preparations for turns from Fourth and Fifth Positions en dehors and en dedans are studied en face at a very slow tempo and later in épaulement, facing corners 2 or 8.

Serebrennikov explains that during a performance, the stage form of the position of the girl's working foot is slightly higher on the mid-calf section of the shin, as opposed to the classroom form of sur le cou-de-pied. At a later time, the working foot may be placed, as some contemporary choreographers prefer, high on the front of the supporting knee or to the side of the supporting knee.

The allongée (elongated) position of both arms in Second Position (as seen in Sketch 15a) during the demi-plié preparation is a Russian aesthetic choice. Some schools prefer the right hand in First Position to be flexed during the demi-plié in Fourth Position. The force of the turn initiated by the left arm from Second Position is not measurably influenced by any of the positions of the right arm.

The boy must observe that some partners will take force for the turn in a characteristic short and sharp plié with a strong force, or with a soft plié and sluggish force. The girl may lean away from the vertical axis for a turn which the boy must correct by putting her on balance. If the force from the girl is sluggish and many pirouettes are required, the boy may give impetus to the turns during the preparatory demi-plié in Fourth Position by slightly changing the line of his hands on her waist in a CONTRARY direction to her turn. Then, at the moment she takes force, he must simultaneously reverse the slight movement of his hands toward the direction of the turn to give her extra impetus, initiating a slight push-pull movement, hands level and equidistant. During the turns, the boy must keep his elbows down and guide the girl's body within the circle between his thumb and forefinger, keeping the other fingers and palm flat on the girl's waist once he has helped to give impetus for the turn. When multiple pirouettes are required, it is usual for one of the boy's hands to follow her turn by helping her to revolve with a light, subtle, repeated pressure from the hand on the side of the direction of the turn. The hand opposite the direction of the turn maintains the balance; the other hand propels the turn. The movements must NEVER be obvious to the audience. The girl must use her head correctly at each revolution as she would in solo dance.

One En Dehors Turn from Fourth Position

After the demi-plié in Fourth Position, the girl takes force and does one turn en dehors with the boy barely touching her waist and NOT moving along her beltline forwards or backwards. He stops the turn by squeezing her waist with both hands and ending in any small or large pose given by the teacher.

One En Dehors Turn from Fifth Position

Using the rules for support as in the turn from Fourth Position, the girl does a demi-plié with the right foot front in Fifth Position. She does a relevé into sur le cou-de-pied devant or derrière and turns en dehors or en dedans ending with a small or large pose. The boy barely touches her waist and does NOT move along her beltline before the turn begins.

Maintaining the Girl's Balance during Multiple Turns

When the girl does three or four turns, the boy must help by shifting his hands along her beltline during her demi-plié in the direction opposite to the direction of the turn before the moment she takes force. He strengthens her turn by the effort of both his hands. The boy, as described above, keeps his hands palms down and keeps her waist within the space between his thumb and index finger on the supporting side. That hand, on the supporting side, seems to be watching the girl's balance and maintaining it, while the other hand, with light pulls in the direction of and during the turn, increases the number of revolutions. A noticeable motion by the boy, however, to pump out more turns is considered bad form.

Once the boy has mastered the principles of partnering multiple turns, he will be able to adjust to any characteristics of a future partner and guide the turns smoothly, elegantly, and expertly.

Executing Multiple En Dehors Turns from an Attitude Croisée Pose

The girl begins the turn standing on the left foot sur la pointe with the right raised to corner 8 at 45 degrees and slightly bent at the knee, less high than in attitude en avant. (Sketch 16. Position for multiple turns from attitude croisée.) The right arm is in First Position, the left arm in Second Position. The boy stands behind her, both hands on the beltline, right slightly forward, left slightly back, and with an energetic effort of both hands, gives the signal to turn as if starting a top by reversing the movement of his hands. The girl at the same time takes force and turns en dehors with the right foot in mid-shin

16. Position for multiple turns from attitude croisée

position. The boy keeps his hand at her waist, following the general rules of support and the principle of maintaining her balance on the supporting side. He lightly pulls in the direction of the turn for multiple turns.

It is useful, says Serebrennikov, to combine this croisée pose with turns from Fourth Position: End a turn from Fourth à la seconde at 90 degrees, then change through passé to the croisée attitude devant and turn en dehors from there, right foot at mid-shin position. Demi-plié may be used in attitude before taking force for the turn en dehors or the girl may remain on pointe after the à la seconde position.

Multiple En Dedans Turns from First Arabesque

The girl assumes a First Arabesque position on the left foot sur la pointe with the boy standing in Second Position or in fondu on the left leg with the right in pointe tendue, holding the girl's waist with both hands. (Sketch 17a. First Arabesque position before a turn.) He then moves his hands along her beltline, right forwards, left backwards, and with the effort of both hands gives the signal to turn as the girl rises to a vertical position. At the same moment, the girl takes force and turns en dedans (to the left) with the right foot strongly whipped into retiré devant as she simultaneously raises her arms to Third Position. (Sketch 17b. Side view of support for a turn en dedans from First Arabesque with both hands.)

The same principles are used when starting a turn in Third Arabesque, boy behind the girl; Fourth Arabesque, with partners face to face; from pose écartée with the girl on her left leg, her back to corner 8 and the boy facing her; in en dehors or en dedans directions with demi-plié before taking force for the turn or without demi-plié.

17a. First Arabesque position
before a turn

17b. Side view of support for a turn en dedans
from First Arabesque with both hands

Multiple En Dehors Turns Approaching the Boy from Arabesque Par Terre Position

The girl faces point 7 standing on the left leg in Second Arabesque par terre (right arm forward, right leg at pointe tendue). The boy stands about two steps behind her in the same position. (Sketch 18a. Preparations in Second Arabesque par terre.) The girl turns to the boy and takes a step on the right foot as tombé or preparation degagé facing the boy. (Sketch 18b. Demi-plié preparation for en dehors turn.) She does a posé onto the pointe of the left foot, raising her arms into Third Position as she turns en dehors. The boy stretches out his right arm palm sideways during her demi-plié and guides her into vertical position as she comes towards him. (Sketch 18c. Position of the en dehors turn.) He supports her turn in a strictly vertical position with his left hand, whole palm at the waist along the beltline.

18a. Preparations in Second Arabesque par terre

18c. Position of the en dehors turn

18b. Demi-plié preparation for en dehors turn

Multiple En Dedans Turns from a Series of Tours En Chaînés

The girl does a series of tours en chaînés along a diagonal line from corner 6 to corner 2 and steps two steps away from the boy into tombé Fourth Position onto her right foot. She then steps onto pointe of the left foot and turns en dehors. The boy meets and supports her in the same manner as in the previous exercises.

Multiple En Dedans Turns from a Series of Turns En Chaînés

After a series of turns or tours en chaînés as in the previous exercise, the girl does a demi-plié in Fourth Position on the left leg and does a posé or relevé onto the pointe of the right foot and turns en dedans. The boy meets and supports her in the same manner with his hand on the waist of the supporting side.

Tour à la Seconde at 90 Degrees

The girl takes a Fourth Position with the right foot forward in croisée position, right arm in First Position, left in Second Position with the boy at her left side at a distance far enough not to touch her raised leg. (Sketch 19. Preparation for tour à la seconde.) The girl does a relevé onto the pointe of her right foot, left à la seconde at 90 degrees as she turns to the right, arms in Third Position. WHEN THE RAISED LEG HAS PASSED THE BOY, he quickly takes a large step toward her, supporting her with both hands at the waist and stops her in a given pose. The finishing pose might be attitude croisée, Second Arabesque, or Third Arabesque. The poses should be practiced with and without demi-plié preparation.

19. Preparation for tour à la seconde

4 · Falling Poses and Promenades

Falling Poses and Positions Using Two Hands

IF THE FALL is to the right, the girl stands in Fifth Position sur les pointes, right croisé devant, épaulement to the right with a lift in the body, and arms in Third Position. The boy stands behind her, arms around her waist, his left hand clasping his right wrist. He then puts his left foot close to her pointes on the LEFT side of her Fifth Position. (Sketch 20a. Starting position for lowering the girl into a fall.) He firmly presses the girl to him and lunges into a deep Fourth Position fondu to point 3 on his right foot, keeping his left foot in place to prevent the girl's feet from slipping as she falls. The girl, without disturbing her position, falls with his lunge, her body close to the floor. (Sketch 20b. Fall to the right.) He returns her to the vertical position with a strong push of his right foot without changing her position. During the fall, as during the return, he must keep her torso firm and straight, bending neither right nor left.

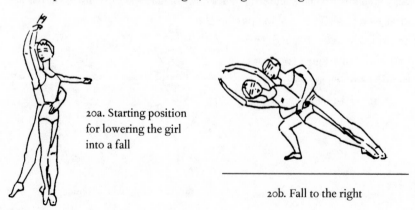

20a. Starting position
for lowering the girl
into a fall

20b. Fall to the right

Falls Back and Front from Fifth Position sur les Pointes

With the girl facing point 7 in the same starting Fifth Position, right foot front, sur les pointes, arms in Third Position, she falls backwards as the boy lunges to point 3. His left foot is in the same bracing position as in the first exercise, with a fall to the side, and his arms are in the same supporting position. (Sketch 21a. Fall backwards from Fifth Position.)

With the girl now facing point 3 and in the same Fifth Position, she falls forward, slightly arching her upper back as the boy lunges to point 3. (Sketch 21b. Fall forward from Fifth Position.) Reverse the exercises with the boy's bracing foot on the right as the girl falls to the left.

21a. Fall backwards from Fifth Position

21b. Fall forwards from Fifth Position

In pas de deux dance, the girl's arms are positioned as in solo work, the only difference being that when the partners take hands, their palms can face upward or downward to adapt to the needs of the particular exercise. The simplest and safest hold with two hands, particularly when the girl's arms are in Second Position, is when the boy stands behind her, palms of his hands over hers, with the tips of his fingers resting just under each of her hands. (Sketch 22. Holding the girl palm to palm.) The boy's hands must not press downward on the girl's arms but must be kept level. Other two-hand holds from various angles are seen in Sketch 23: palm to palm with partners facing opposite

22. Holding the girl palm to palm

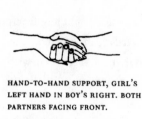

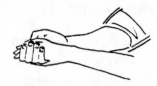

HAND-TO-HAND
SUPPORT IN 2ND
POSITION. BOTH
PARTNERS FACING
FRONT.

HAND-TO-HAND SUPPORT, GIRL'S
LEFT HAND IN BOY'S RIGHT. BOTH
PARTNERS FACING FRONT.

HAND-TO-HAND
SUPPORT IN 2ND
POSITION. BOTH
PARTNERS FACING
ONE ANOTHER.

HAND-TO-HAND SUPPORT, GIRL'S
RIGHT HAND IN BOY'S LEFT. PARTNERS
FACING OPPOSITE DIRECTIONS.

HAND-TO-HAND
SUPPORT IN 2ND
POSITION. PARTNERS
FACING OPPOSITE
DIRECTIONS.

23. Several holds from various angles

directions; support in Second Position, both partners facing front; support in Second Position, both partners facing one another; support clasping the wrists, partners facing opposite directions; Sketch 24a: two-hand hold in arabesque; and Sketch 24b: wrist/forearm hold in attitude croisée.

The girl may be supported by the elbows of both arms. This hold is basically not different from supporting her by the wrists. Regardless of what support is used, the boy should always maintain the girl's conventional, classical hand positions as nearly as possible.

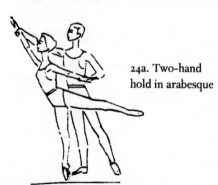

24a. Two-hand
hold in arabesque

24b. Wrist/
forearm hold in
attitude croisée

Basic 360 Degree Turn Supported by Both Hands

The partners face each other with the girl's back to the audience. The girl is on her right foot sur la pointe, the left is sur le cou-de-pied derrière. Both partners hold their right hands palm-to-palm in Third Position and their left arms in First Position. (Sketch 25a. Starting position for a two-hand turn.) The turn is accomplished in three movements:

1. The boy, who is standing in a modified Second Position, opens their left arms from First Position into Second Position keeping their right arms in Third. (Sketch 25b. Half turn to the girl's right.)
2. The boy then opens their right arms from Third Position to Second Position as the girl faces front. (Sketch 25c. Partners with Second Position arms.) He then moves their left arms slowly into Third Position. (Sketch 25d. Left arms in Third Position.)
3. As the final move of the full turn, their right arms move from Second Position to First Position, and the girl faces the boy once more, left arms in Third Position, right arms in First Position. (Sketch 25e. End of full turn changing arm positions.)

A full turn has been executed, and there has been an exchange of arm positions. The girl helps the turn by slightly moving the heel of her supporting foot in the direction of the turn while maintaining the turn-out and keeping her cen-

| 25a. Starting position for a two-hand turn | 25b. Half turn to the girl's right | 25c. Partners with Second Position arms | 25d. Left arms in Third Position | 25e. End of full turn changing arm position |

ter of balance over her supporting pointe. The turn should be reversed, practiced slowly until smooth, and may then increase in uninterrupted speed.

Principle for Promenades

In promenades using both hands, the boy walks with ordinary steps around the girl in a part or a whole circle, the center of which is the pointe of the girl's supporting foot. As described earlier, if the girl's turn is to the left, his first step is made with the right foot; if her turn is to the right, he begins the walk with his left foot. The girl helps by pivoting the heel of the supporting foot in the direction of the turn. In the walk, the heel of the boy's working foot is placed directly in front of the toe of the supporting foot and continues in that manner. After finding the correct balance for the pose by using the outer foot first, the boy maintains the exact circumference of the circle throughout the turn. Promenades are studied first in a slow tempo without changing the girl's pose and then with changes of pose during the walk.

Promenade in Attitude with Two-hand Support

The boy stands in effacé with his weight firmly centered over his right leg, left stretched backward on the ball of his foot. His right arm is stretched forward, his left arm in Second Position, palm upward, and his head is turned left toward the girl. The girl takes attitude effacée on right pointe, placing her left hand on the boy's hand and her right on his left shoulder. Once her balance is stable, the boy straightens his right leg and slowly begins a circle to the left, beginning with the right foot.

Prior to a promenade, the girl usually begins with a pas glissade, pas couru, or a simple step onto pointe in attitude. The girl must place herself into a pose at a distance that will enable her to maintain the pose with outstretched arms and without bending excessively at the elbow during the turn. (Sketch 26. Promenade in attitude with two-hand support.) The promenade should be practiced using other poses as well as with the boy walking backwards, outer foot making the first step of the circle.

26. Promenade in attitude
with two-hand support

Promenade in Attitude Using a Cradle Hold

The boy holds the girl by cradling one arm around her waist with the other holding her hand. (Sketch 27. Promenade in attitude with cradle hold.) The girl stands in attitude de face on the left pointe. The boy is at her left side, standing on the left leg with the right in a modified tendu back. He cradles his right arm around the back of her body so that the tips of his fingers rest on the front of her right hip. He holds her outstretched left hand in his left. The boy brings his legs together and circles to the right. During the promenade he must not straighten his left elbow but must remain close to the girl, controlling the line of her hips and allowing her neither to lose her balance nor to deviate from the circle or pose. As a variation, the boy may place his right hand on the girl's hip. (Sketch 28. Variation of promenade in attitude with hip hold.)

27. Promenade in attitude
with cradle hold

28. Variation of promenade in
attitude with a hip hold

Promenade à la Seconde with Palm-to-Palm Hold

The girl stands with her back to point 1 in Fifth Position sur les pointes, right foot devant, arms in Third Position. The boy faces her, arms in Second Position, palms upward. The girl opens her arms to Second and places her hands on his as she does a développé at 90 degrees with the right leg. (Sketch 29. Promenade à la seconde with two-hand hold.) Before beginning the promenade, the boy must turn his hips slightly to the left in the line his circle will take. However, he must keep his shoulders facing the girl, and both boy and girl must hold their arms firmly in Second and maintain the space between them.

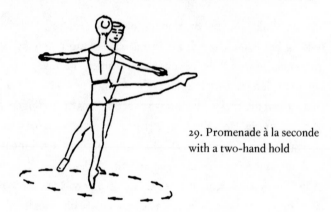

29. Promenade à la seconde with a two-hand hold

5 · Three Basic Turns

WHEN THE PROMENADE à la seconde has been properly mastered and the partners are able to finish in the same well placed position in which they started, a turn from this position is simply a matter of taking force and quickly bringing the working leg from à la seconde position to sur le cou-de-pied or retiré front. The girl must take care not to include extraneous movements that will displace the hip or knee such as whipping or fouetté movements. Sufficient force, created by swiftly bending the knee and using the arms correctly, will produce multiple turns as follows:

Pirouette en Dehors after Completing a Promenade à la Seconde at 90 Degrees

These pirouettes go straight into an en dehors or en dedans turn, without a stop from a stabilized à la seconde position after completing the promenade, and may be executed with or without a fondu (demi-plié). The girl takes force by pushing away from the boy's hands, palms to palms, and raising her arms to Third Position. At the same time, the boy lightly but firmly guides the girl's arms upwards and then quickly places both hands on her waist as she completes her pirouette.

Pirouette à la Seconde at 90 Degrees Holding the Girl's Wrists

This exercise can be studied two ways: The boy may stand behind the girl, or he can face her. The girl faces point 1 on left pointe à la seconde at 90 degrees.

The boy stands behind her, holding her wrists in both hands from below, palms upwards. With her right leg, the girl swings slightly to the left, opposite the turn that will be to the right, pushes away from the boy's hands, takes force, and turns en dehors with her right leg remaining in à la seconde position. After the boy has helped her take force, he takes a big step backwards and as soon as the girl's raised leg passes him, he quickly steps forward again and catches her by the waist or by the hands. During the turn, the girl either changes her arms into Third Position or she may keep them in Second Position. If the boy faces the girl at the start of the turn, it is more usual for the turn to be en dedans using the same method.

Pirouette en Dehors from Pose Croisée Devant

The girl faces corner 8 on the left foot with the right in attitude croisée, her right arm in First Position, left in Second Position. The boy stands behind her holding her beltline. (Sketch 30. Preparatory position before pirouette en dehors from pose croisée devant.) With the effort of both of his hands as a signal, he gives a push for the turn. The girl, at the same time, places her arms in First Position during the turn, her right foot at the front of the shinbone of the supporting leg. During the turn, the boy guides the pirouette holding the girl's waist, finishing in attitude croisée devant or in any other given pose.

Serebrennikov again emphasizes the need for mastery of each exercise and the importance of a "common tempo" to assure the quality and number of turns. At the beginning of the study, the boy must not give too strong a push with his hands to increase the force of turns.

30. Preparatory position before pirouette en dehors from pose croisée devant

Pirouette en Dedans from Attitude with Both Hands on the Boy's Arm

The girl is in attitude effacée on right pointe, her left hand on the boy's left wrist, her right on his shoulder. The boy does a lunge in Fourth Position toward corner 2, right foot forward and is slightly in front of the girl, effacée position. His right arm is in Second Position, palms up or down; his head is turned to the left toward the girl. (Sketch 31. Preparatory position for pirouette en dedans from attitude effacée.) The girl swings her left foot to Second Position at 45 degrees and quickly bends her knee so that her left foot is in sur le cou-de-pied front for the turn en dedans. Her arms go from the boy's wrist and shoulder up to Third Position. After she takes force for the turn, the boy rises from the lunge and takes a big step to be behind her and at her side while he supports her during the turn with both hands at her waist. The turn may end in various poses and positions.

31. Preparatory position for pirouette en dedans from attitude effacée

Pirouette from First Arabesque Holding the Girl's Wrists

The boy stands behind the girl on his right foot, arabesque à terre, holding her wrists in both hands. The girl stands in First Arabesque, right arm in Third, left arm straight and back. (Sketch 32a. Position for an en dedans turn with wrist hold.) With his left hand, the boy gives her strength to commence the turn, as she places her left arm in Preparatory Position for the turn. (Sketch 32b. Position for the turn). During the pirouette, he holds her right wrist softly, allowing her to turn easily and, at the same time, to maintain her weight over her sup-

32a. Position for an en dedans turn with wrist hold

32b. Position for the turn

porting leg. If the girl finishes her pirouette in First Arabesque, the boy must catch her left wrist as she opens it to the back and finishes the turn.

In the turn position, the girl may change arms as she turns, in which case the boy will release her right wrist and immediately take her left. This change of hands takes place when the girl's arms are in Third. This turn may also be practiced in a low attitude. The boy in this instance moves a little away from the girl, but without disturbing her balance or displacing her raised arms.

En Dedans Turn from Arabesque Position

The boy kneels on his right knee facing point 7, arms in Second Position, palms up. The girl faces and approaches him from a short distance with a walk or running steps and takes an arabesque on the right foot, placing both her hands on his palms. The girl must calculate her approach so that during her turn, he can hold her with both hands on her waist without bending forward. (Sketch 33a. Preparatory position for turn en dedans from arabesque.) The girl may do a penchée or remain upright. From the upright position, she pushes away from the boy's hands, takes force, and makes a turn en dedans by moving her left foot quickly from arabesque to Second Position at 45 degrees and then swiftly bending the knee to sur le cou-de-pied front for the turn. Her arms move from Sec-

33a. Preparatory position for turn
en dedans from arabesque

33b. Position for the en dedans
turn from arabesque

ond Position to Third Position for the turn as the boy supports her with both his hands at her waist during the turn and remains on the knee. (Sketch 33b. Position for the en dedans turn from arabesque.)

Pirouette en Dehors with Girl Holding the Boy's Middle Finger

The girl faces corner 8 on the left foot, with the right foot in sur le cou-de-pied front. Her left arm is in Second Position, palm resting on the boy's left palm. Her right arm is in Third Position with her hand holding the boy's middle finger. (Sketch 34. Direction of boy's finger into girl's hand for finger turn.) The boy stands behind her, right arm above and slightly in front of her head. His left hand holds her left hand in Second Position. The girl extends her right foot slightly forward at 45 degrees and takes force by swiftly placing her foot back into sur le cou-de-pied and pushing strongly away from the boy's left hand with her left hand. At the same time, she changes into First Position with her left hand where it may remain or move into preparatory position for the turn. During the turn, she continues to loosely clasp the boy's finger, encircling it with her right hand but never fully straightening her arm. When the turns are finished, the boy catches the girl's left arm by the wrist and helps her assume an ending pose. As in multiple turns where the boy pushes in a subtle manner for more turns, he may also use the finger turn to increase the number of turns by pushing his finger within the circle of the girl's hand. Once again, this is not a recommended practice, and if used, must never be seen by the audience. The boy must maintain a strong arm in Second for the girl to give a sufficient push while taking force to increase the number of turns.

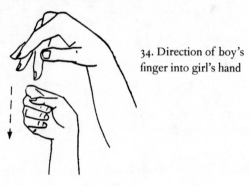

34. Direction of boy's finger into girl's hand

6 · Finding the Point of Balance in Falling and Rising

SEREBRENNIKOV gives us the principle for two falls from one leg supported by the wrists; a fall from Fifth Position supported by the wrist and waist; and a movement that begins on the floor and ends on one leg with hand-to-hand support.

Maintaining the Support during a Fall and Recovery in First Arabesque with Wrist Support

The boy stands behind the girl who is in First Arabesque on right pointe and holds her wrists. After the girl's balance has been established, the boy braces the fall by placing his left foot to the left of her supporting right pointe and does a fondu on the LEFT leg, extending the right leg with the heel on the floor, foot toward point 3. His left arm is tightly pressed against the left side of his chest, and as she descends over the arch of her foot to the floor, she leads the movement with the right hip and then bends to the left from the waist. The boy raises her right arm and his own, but not as high as Third Position, toward point 3. (Sketch 35. Lowering the girl into a falling position holding her wrists.)

35. Lowering the girl into a falling position holding her wrists

The recovery is initiated by the boy with a sharp and steady pull of both arms and a strong push from his left leg as he pulls the girl toward him into First Arabesque and draws his right foot back to his left. The girl must not allow her legs to slacken, and the boy must be conscious of recentering his weight as he pulls her back into First Arabesque.

This fall may also be performed with the partners' hands palm to palm. (Sketch 36. The palm-to-palm position of the partners' hands.) (Sketch 37. Lowering the girl into a falling position holding the palms of her hands.)

After the fall, the girl must always return to First Arabesque. The boy may let go of her left hand as she closes in Fifth sur les pointes.

36. The palm-to-palm position of the partners' hands

37. Lowering the girl into a falling position holding her hands

Maintaining the Support by Both Hands While Lowering the Girl onto the Boy's Back

The partners face one another, arms in Second Position palm to palm with the girl facing point 3. She steps into attitude croisée on the left pointe. The boy faces point 7 standing on the left leg with the right leg in battement tendu derrière. (Sketch 38a. Starting position for lowering from attitude croisée.) With his right arm, the boy leads the girl's left arm up to Third Position as he draws her right arm into Preparatory Position. At that moment, the girl brings her right to sur le cou-de-pied devant position and turns toward the left en dedans. As the movement continues, the boy moves his left arm from Preparatory Position into Second Position toward point 1 and, still holding palm-to-palm, turns his body to the right without ducking during the transition or making an obvious change. The partners end back to back. The girl's left arm remains in Third Position. As the girl's right knee passes him, he places his left foot BEHIND her supporting left leg, and they press tightly back to back. The girl looks toward point 1. (Sketch 38b. Completion of turn before the fall backwards.)

The girl ends the movement with a développé devant, her right leg at 90 degrees as the boy supports and lowers her on his back in a smooth deep lunge toward point 3. (Sketch 38c. Fall position in développé devant.)

The return is accomplished with a strong push backwards from the boy's right leg as he assumes an upright position and gives the girl a stable position in any given pose. It is important to remember that the line of the left leg and hip must be kept straight during the lunge and the return.

38a. Starting position for lowering from attitude croisée

38b. Completion of turn before the fall backwards

38c. Fall position in développé devant

Maintaining the Support at the Waist and Wrist during a Fall and Recovery in Fifth Position

The boy stands behind the girl who is in Fifth Position, right foot devant with her right arm in Third Position and her left in Second Position. The boy holds the wrist of her right hand with his right hand and cradles her waist with his left arm, fingers touching her right hip. (Sketch 39a. Starting position for waist and wrist support for a fall from Fifth Position.) His left foot braces the SIDE of her left foot when she rises to sur les pointes. He then turns the girl to face point 3 and smoothly lunges toward point 3 on his right foot. Simultaneously, both boy and girl stretch their right arms forward as he lowers her to the fall pose and they both bend slightly backwards. (Sketch 39b. Fall position with wrist and waist support.) During this movement, both partners must feel the mutual level of their shoulders firmly maintained at close contact. In lowering into and returning from this fall, the boy's right arm is as important as his left. The girl must be returned to her original position as in the previous exercise.

A variation of this fall may begin from First Arabesque or attitude effacée. The exercise should be practiced without holding the girl's wrist.

Another variation has the girl in Fifth Position, right foot devant, arms in Third. The boy stands behind her holding her left wrist in his left hand. He places his left foot by the girl's pointes, and his right arm cradles her body so that his fingers reach her left hip. He turns the girl toward point 3 and lunges in the same direction onto his right foot with his left hand still holding her left wrist. The girl is in the same position as in the previous exercise, but the boy's arms are differently placed.

Still another variation has the girl in First Arabesque on her right foot. The boy stands behind her holding her wrists in both hands. He releases her left

39a. Starting position for waist
and wrist support for a fall from
Fifth Position

39b. Fall position with wrist and
waist support

hand as she brings her left foot into Fifth devant and her arms into Third, making a half turn so that her back is to point 3. He firmly places his left arm around her waist and, bracing his left foot against her pointe, lunges toward point 3, lowering the girl backwards.

The principle of releasing the girl's hand and turning her in a vertical position is the same as that used in all falling exercises.

Holds with One Hand

All the movements studied earlier using two hands on the waist must now be repeated in the following sequence: support by one hand to one hand; support of one hand on the wrist; support of one hand squeezing the waist; support of one arm encircling the waist; or any combination of these supports. The boy must remember that the girl's body will incline toward the side away from the working leg. He must help her control her balance and guide her body in the necessary direction. In all such situations, the girl must control the movements of her arms very strictly.

Maintaining the Support during a Rise from the Floor to a Pose on One Foot with Hand-to-Hand Support

The girl stands in Fifth Position, right foot devant in effacée position, facing corner 2. From this position, she bends her knees and lowers herself onto her left knee, continuing the movement backwards until she is sitting on the floor with her right leg extended toward corner 2. Her right arm is in First Position; her left arm is in Second Position, both palms face down. The left shoulder is turned slightly toward corner 8, and there is a slight lean backwards. The boy takes a deep lunge on his left leg toward corner 6 and offers his right hand to the girl with a gracious gesture. She lowers her right hand onto his hand. (Sketch 40a. Floor position before the rise to attitude effacée.) He gives a light, almost invisible pull as a signal, and the girl quickly pushes off the floor onto her left knee, continuing the movement onto a straight right leg into First Arabesque or attitude effacée. (Sketch 40b. Attitude effacée position in rise from the floor with hand-to-hand support.) During this movement, the boy has energetically moved from the deep lunge into a vertical pose by taking a large step backwards onto his right leg and ending in left tendu back. His right arm from hand to shoulder must remain rigid, and the girl must hold her right shoulder down firmly.

Serebrennikov admonishes the teacher to vary the exercises as much as possible, increasing complication to develop deftness, quick orientation, and adaptability to combinations that will be met on stage.

40a. Floor position before the rise to attitude effacée

40b. Attitude effacée position in rise from the floor with hand-to-hand support

7 · Promenades and One-hand Turns

SEREBRENNIKOV reminds us that the principle for a movement remains the same despite the degree of difficulty of the exercise. Mastery of each principle is essential and follows logically upon mastery of the preceding principle. This chapter gives us the technique required for those smooth and quiet moments of pas de deux dance in which one pose melds into another with apparent ease.

Basic 360 Degree Turn from a Static Position
Holding One Hand

The boy faces point 1 as the girl faces him with her back to point 1. She stands on her right pointe with the left sur le cou-de-pied derrière. Her right arm is in Third Position, palm turned toward the boy, left arm in Preparatory Position. The boy takes her right hand with his right hand, palm to palm. His left arm is opened to the side but not in a definite Second Position. The boy gives a signal to turn with a slight but smooth and firm movement of his right hand. During the turn, the girl's right arm is kept in Third Position slightly in front of the crown of her head. When the girl begins to turn, the boy makes a gliding movement, and turns his right wrist edgewise into the turn and over their joined palms. As the turn reaches the halfway position with both arms in Second Position, the girl has slightly loosened her grip to allow the boy's hand to glide around hers, without moving her arm backward or forward, until his hand has circled her hand without letting it go. The girl must strive to make the turn independently, barely touching the boy's hand and using her supporting foot actively by turning the heel in the direction of the turn.

The counterclockwise motion of the boy's hand ends when the turn is completed, and he stops the turn by holding the girl's hand tightly, palm to palm once more. The turn must be practiced to the other side.

A 360 Degree Turn from a Static Pose with Palm-to-Palm Support

The starting position of the partners is the same as in the previous exercise except that the boy's left arm is in First Position, palm up in front of the girl, while the girl's hand is palm down when they join hands. The boy then opens his right arm to the right into Second Position thereby turning the girl half a turn so that she has her back to him. With a sharp movement, he raises both their right arms to Third Position overhead and makes a strong movement with his wrist to complete the turn. Their palms remain tightly pressed during the turn which ends, as it began, with the arms in First Position. The boy stops the turn with a slight squeeze of his hand. Consecutive turns to the left side should also be practiced. This turn requires a strong, steady movement from the boy's wrist, along with a pivot by the girl on her supporting pointe.

A half or three-quarter turn with the boy holding the girl with one hand on the waist begins with the girl in attitude croisée on her left pointe. The boy, standing by her left shoulder with his right arm over her body, holds her from the right side to the center of her waist. He turns her to the left and moves backwards, trying to remain behind her left shoulder. She finishes in First Arabesque.

The boy could also hold the girl's right hip, bringing the upper side of his forearm downwards and slightly forwards as extra support.

Promenades

Promenades may be studied in all basic poses. The girl's hand holding the boy's may be in First, Second or Third Positions. Her arm must be held firmly still with a straight line running through the center of the bones from shoulder to elbow to wrist at any level and whether or not the arm is bent or straight. It must not move during the promenade.

Promenade en Attitude with Girl Holding
Both Hands on the Boy's Arm

The boy stands in Fourth, weight firmly on his right leg, left stretched backwards on the ball of his foot. His right arm is stretched forward and placed on
her right shoulder, his left is in Third, his head turned to the right. (Sketch 41.
Preparation for promenade in attitude with interlocking arms.) The girl takes
attitude effacée on right pointe, placing her right hand on the boy's right shoulder and her left arm in Third Position. When the girl's balance is stabilized, the
boy, beginning with the right foot, slowly circles to the left. The girl may begin
the movement with a glissade, pas couru, or a simple step toward the boy. This
promenade should be studied using large and small poses and should maintain
air and light between the partners as they move.

41. Preparation for promenade in   42. First Arabesque ending with
attitude with interlocking arms   boy holding girl's right hip

An Incomplete Turn from a Static Pose on One Foot
with One-Hand Support at the Waist

The girl stands on the left pointe in attitude croisée. The boy stands behind her
left shoulder holding her with his right hand over her body and around the
waist from the right side as far as the center. He turns the girl to the left and at
the same time steps backwards, staying behind her left shoulder. She finishes
the turn in Fourth Arabesque. (Sketch 42. Fourth Arabesque ending with boy
holding girl's right hip.) If the movement of the boy's hand is not enough to

turn the girl, he may shift his hand with a gliding movement along her beltline in the direction OPPOSITE the turn for more force. The Fourth Arabesque is stopped by a squeeze of the boy's hand on the right side of the girl's waist. Then, the entire movement is practiced to the left. The promenade may also be performed with the boy's hand on the girl's hip.

Promenades

1. The girl steps into attitude effacée on right pointe. The boy, facing the girl, offers his right hand, palm upwards. She places her right hand on his, arm in First Position. In this position, the boy promenades around her to the right. His steps must be smooth and equidistant. During this promenade, she must hold her pose without moving. Promenades should be studied slowly and incorporated into different enchaînements.

2. The girl stands in First Arabesque on her right pointe. The boy stands on his left foot, right foot pointe tendue derrière, and takes her right wrist in his right hand. (Sketch 43. First Arabesque holding the girl's wrist.) He circles to the left, or, if he holds the girl's left wrist, circles to the right.

3. The girl stands écarté devant or derrière on her left pointe. The boy stands slightly behind and to her left on his left foot, right pointe tendue à la seconde, and holds her right wrist in his right hand. Her left arm is in Second, in front of and across the boy's chest. (Sketch 44. Pose écarté

43. First Arabesque holding the girl's right wrist

44. Pose écartée holding the girl's right wrist

holding the girl's right wrist.) In this position, the boy must move directly behind and around the girl's spine to help her maintain her weight directly over her supporting leg. This is a difficult promenade.

4. This promenade has the boy use the same principles as those stated above. The girl stands in First Arabesque on her left pointe. The boy places the palm of his right hand firmly on her right hip at waist level and stands so that his left foot is directly in the same line as her supporting toe and waist. (Sketch 45. First Arabesque with boy holding the girl's right hip with his right hand.) The boy's right foot is pointe tendue derrière. From this pose, the girl performs a grand port de bras devant. As she begins to lean downwards, the boy slightly directs her body forwards, taking care not to disturb her balance. Her movement depends entirely upon her ability to tilt her pelvis over her supporting leg without arching her spine. He can only help her to maintain a perpendicular supporting leg.

During port de bras, the girl's pose should acquire elegance and lightness. She must retain the pose throughout the promenade, while the boy concentrates on keeping her weight centered over her supporting leg.

The practice at first should not be full promenade. Promenades should also be practiced in Second, Third, and Fourth Arabesques and attitudes. (Sketch 46. Promenade in Fourth Arabesque with girl held by the boy's right hand on her waist.)

45. First Arabesque with boy holding the girl's right hip with his right hand

46. Promenade in Fourth Arabesque with girl held by the boy's right hand on her waist

Another aspect of a hold around and behind the waist begins with the girl in attitude croisée on her right pointe, her arms in Third. The boy faces her with his right arm curved around the back of her waist, fingertips reaching her right side, elbow slightly bent. He stands on his right foot, left in pointe tendue derrière with his body and head held slightly backwards. The boy then lowers the girl away from himself as if she were resting on his arm. (Sketch 47. Attitude croisée with the boy's right hand around and behind the girl's waist.) In this position, the boy may circle by stepping forwards or backwards. At first, only a half circle should be attempted. Later, a full circle and ultimately three, four, or more may be mastered. At the end of the promenade, the boy must return the girl to her original pose and help her regain her weight over her own center of balance.

During a promenade in écarté, when the boy has one arm around the girl's waist, the partners must feel only one point of contact. During all promenades where the boy holds the girl with one hand or has his arm on or around her body, he must never contract his fingers strongly nor hold her costume. Whether his hand is over or under her body, a well opened stretch between thumb and forefinger embracing the side of the girl's waist is a correct position. The actual position always depends upon the girl's pose. In some promenades, the partners face each other in the following position: the palm of the girl's right hand rests on the boy's right shoulder, and his right palm rests on her right shoulder. (Sketch 48. Interlocking arms in attitude effacée.)

47. Attitude croisée with the boy's right hand around and behind the girl's waist

48. Interlocking arms in attitude effacée

Pirouettes

1. The girl stands in attitude effacée on her right pointe. The boy faces her holding her right hand in his right, palm to palm, in First Position. The girl does a fondu, rises sur la pointe, and takes force for a pirouette en dedans. At the moment their hands join, the boy's right arm must be strong and resilient. The girl pushes away from his hand and begins to turn as he immediately places both hands on her waist and helps her to regain and retain her center of balance during the pirouette. These pirouettes should be practiced with and without the preliminary fondu.

Pirouette from First Arabesque

The girl is in high First Arabesque on her right pointe, facing point 3. One step away, the boy stands or kneels facing her and holds both hands or her right wrist with his right hand. His pose is on the left leg, right in battement tendu derrière, left arm in modified Second. The girl does a pirouette en dedans with the left foot in sur le cou-de-pied devant, raising both arms or her right arm to Third and lowering her left into Preparatory Position. At the moment she takes force, the boy leads her right arm over her head into Third Position as smoothly and strongly as possible, so that she may raise her body into the vertical position and become balanced. When the girl takes force, the boy's arm must be strongly resilient as she pushes away from him. He may take the girl's waist for the turn. At the moment when the turn begins he must never squeeze the girl's wrist. Her arm must be free to turn in his hand. (Sketch 49. Preparation for tour en dedans from Arabesque Penchée and turn position.) In pirouettes holding the girl's wrist, the boy may either face or stand behind the girl.

Pirouettes with Girl Revolving around
the Boy's Middle Finger

(If more comfortable, the index rather than the middle finger may be used.)

The basic principle for these pirouettes is executed as discussed earlier, but if the girl has already placed her arm above her head before the pirouette be-

49. Preparation for tour en dedans from Arabesque Penchée and turn position

gins and if the boy is already standing behind her holding her arm or hand, then before she begins her pirouette, the boy must rearrange his and her fingers so that his middle finger points downwards and her fingers encircle it.

These pirouettes may be studied beginning with a step, a tombé, pas de bourrée, or other movement as preparation. The girl must finish in all small and large poses. If she remains sur la pointe, without fondu, the boy as a rule can help her by taking her free arm or hand or by placing his free arm on her waist.

Pirouette and Turn in Attitude with a Hold at the Waist

The girl stands à la seconde at 90 degrees on her left pointe, arms in Second. The boy, standing to her right and facing point 1, takes her right hand in his left, palm to palm. With a fondu on the left foot, the girl pushes away from the boy's hand to take force and makes a pirouette en dehors into attitude, raising her arms to Third. The girl should make this turn on her own. The boy then takes a step forwards toward her on his right foot and when her left shoulder approaches him, he may place his right hand behind her body. She opens her left arm into Second and places it around the back of his shoulder. The boy must not stop her pirouette but quickly ensure its continuity by moving forwards in a promenade circle so that the girl can finish in attitude effacée. (Sketch 50a.

Tour from preparatory Second Position.) (Sketch 50b. Tour in attitude with the boy's right arm cradled around the back of the girl's waist, her left arm around his shoulder.) Once the boy has embraced the girl as above, he can turn two, three, or more times; the girl's arm, bent at the elbow, can rest on the boy's right shoulder; she can make a half turn by herself, and then the boy can embrace her waist.

In this type of pirouette the boy must always approach the girl with care and never bump into her, thus spoiling the axis of her turn. He must move speedily into the circle and at the same tempo with the girl. They must coordinate the circling walk without distorting the general line both are making.

50a. Tour from preparatory Second Position

50b. Tour in attitude with the boy's right arm cradled around the back of the girl's waist, her left arm around his shoulder

8 · Three Easy Lifts

SEREBRENNIKOV continues the study of partnering with three examples of slow descents and introduces the exciting study of aerial partnering with three easy lifts.

Maintaining the Support during a Fall and Recovery
in First Arabesque with Hand-to-Hand Support

The girl stands in First Arabesque on her left pointe. The boy stands behind her in an easy Second Position holding her left wrist with his left hand. He tightly holds and presses her right hand close to his chest. The boy braces the instep of his right foot against the girl's left pointe. As he bends his right knee in fondu and stretches his left leg outwards, his body inclines slightly backwards as the girl stretches away from him. At the same time, he releases her left arm and stretches his right arm diagonally downwards and across his chest. His elbow must move slowly and strongly outwards. (Sketch 51. Lowering the girl to the floor with one-hand support.)

The recovery is made with the boy drawing the girl's right arm strongly and smoothly backwards, reversing the way he stretched for the fall. When the girl has returned to arabesque, he can place his two hands on her waist or on her wrists or hands.

51. Lowering the girl to the floor with one-hand support

*Maintaining the Support at the Waist with One Hand in a Fall
in First Arabesque while Lowering the Girl onto the Boy's Side*

The boy stands to the left side of the girl, facing point 1 in an easy Second Position. She is à la seconde as in sketch 50a. She closes her right leg and changes to First Arabesque on her left pointe as he supports her with his right hand around her waist with the tips of his fingers touching her right hip bone. His left hand is extended toward point 7, not quite in a Second Position, palm down. He braces her pointe by placing his right foot directly in FRONT of her left pointe. The girl leans into her left hip and onto the boy's right hip. The boy makes a deep lunge toward point 7 and supports her fall, turning his head to the left to harmonize with the girl's pose. (Sketch 52a. Placement for fall with one hand at the waist.) There must be a straight line from the boy's right foot through his leg and body to support her descent, and the girl must maintain a strong arabesque position. (Sketch 52b. Straight line from foot through leg and body to support the descent.)

The recovery to the First Arabesque is begun by the boy pushing off with the left leg back into the easy Second Position, closer to Sixth or parallel position.

52a. Placement for fall with one
hand at the waist

52b. Straight line from foot
through leg and body to support
the descent

Maintaining Hand-to-Hand Support during a Fall with Both Partners Descending

The partners both face point 1 with the girl to the right of the boy. She places her left arm behind the boy's right forearm as both of them bend elbows and join hands, her left palm in his right palm, edges of the hands downward. The girl's right arm and the boy's left arm are in Preparatory Position. (Sketch 53a. Preparatory position for the fall by both partners.) The girl rises onto pointe in Fifth Position, right foot devant, and the boy places his right foot directly next to the girl's pointes and brings his left foot parallel to his right foot. The partners then carefully and slowly maintain a balance as the girl opens her arms from Preparatory Position to Second Position. (Sketch 53b. Fall with the boy maintaining the bent elbow position close to his chest during the descent.) They both begin to lean away from each other without bending their bodies. The boy slowly extends his right arm into Second Position until both partners are in a balanced falling position. (Sketch 53c. Final balanced position.)

To return to starting position, the boy makes a sharp pull with his right arm at the same time that he places his left foot half a step away from his right foot;

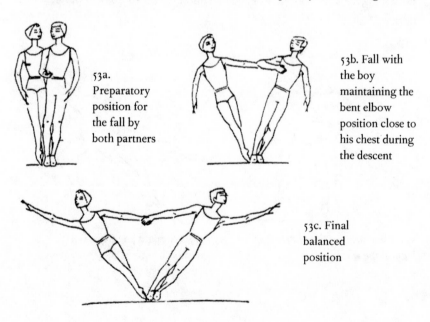

53a. Preparatory position for the fall by both partners

53b. Fall with the boy maintaining the bent elbow position close to his chest during the descent

53c. Final balanced position

he quickly supports the girl with both hands at her waist as they return to a vertical position or to a given pose. Serebrennikov adds that the boy must strive to keep his hands in a natural position throughout the movement.

Lowering the Girl in First Arabesque from One Hand

The girl stands in First Arabesque on her left pointe. The boy is close behind her, the upturned palm of his right hand holding the downturned palm of her right. His right elbow is bent and his forearm is at waist level, left arm in a modified Second. The boy then braces the instep of his right foot against the girl's left pointe. As he bends his right knee in fondu and stretches his left leg outwards and diagonally forwards, his body inclines backwards to balance the girl as she stretches away from him. At the same time, he stretches his right arm diagonally downwards and across his chest. His elbow must stretch slowly and coordinate with the outward stretching of his left leg as the girl descends. Both partners look to the left at the final pose. (Sketch 54. Final pose lowering the girl in First Arabesque from one hand.)

Before giving us the first easy lift in the study of aerial support, Serebrennikov gives us a goal:

> In the process of study, the partners must develop an inner tempo which is reached through harmonious coordination and mutual preparedness and is totally subordinated to the musical tempo. The teacher must protect the boy, especially if he is growing, from injury and trauma as much as possible dur-

54. Final pose lowering the girl in First Arabesque from one hand

ing the study. The lessons must be well thought out and a thorough explanation of the material given with patience. If the combination includes a new method of support, the teacher must give the explanation of the movement first to the girl, then to the boy, since his movements, as a rule, depend upon her movements. After a careful explanation, each pair of partners should perform the exercise separately.

Strict discipline in class must be maintained because injury most often is the result of inattention or lengthy combinations performed with excessive speed, overloaded with complicated lifts, and repeated more than two or three times. One must not allow students to practice difficult lifts or throws (a toss of the girl into the air) without the teacher being present.

A spotter in the form of another student or teacher, one who stands nearby during the execution of a new lift to prevent injury to head or body in case of a fall, provides insurance. It might be wise to keep an ice pack in the studio to place on the injured part should a fall occur.

Because the lower back and knees are most vulnerable to injury during lifts and big jumps, during practice sessions, students should be forbidden to lift on the basis of sheer physical strength. Utilizing the girl's jump, with a limited expenditure of strength displaying a minimum of effort, should be taught. During lifts to the chest or shoulder, or with outstretched arms, the boy must bend his body at the waist while keeping his back straight at all times and his weight centered.

Lifts may be comfortable, uncomfortable, heavy but comfortable, and light but uncomfortable. The ideal partner for a comfortable lift is a girl who has had good professional training, has mastered the forms and technique of classical dance to a high level, is bold, adroit, deft, and trusting of her partner, and who orients herself quickly to any difficult situation. During the lesson she performs the material with the utmost exactitude, according to the rules of classical solo dance. Her muscles are developed properly to facilitate the most complicated lifts.

While in a lift in which the boy's arms are outstretched, the girl must NEVER attempt to adjust or improve her pose independently or to find her own balance. A signal to lift or spring should be unseen by the audience.

The quality of the partnership in aerial support is in the ability of the partners to begin and coordinate their movements together. The girl must calculate her approach and not overjump her partner's position. The trajectory must end exactly at his arms, shoulder, or chest as the lift may require. All this eases the heavy physical load that the boy must carry in aerial dance.

The study of lifts begins with small jumps and small lifts to the level of the chest and shoulder. The jumps are studied in the sequence they are learned in solo dance: jumps from two feet to two feet; from two feet to one foot; from one foot to the other foot; and from one foot to the same foot.

Small Jumps and Lifts to the Level of the Chest or Shoulder

This study includes temps levés sautés, changements de pieds, assemblés, jetés, jetés entrelacés, sissonnes, sissonnes fermées, sissonnes fondues, soubresauts, pas de chat, pas de basque, cabrioles and other small jumps.

The boy may hold the girl with both hands on her waist, by her hands, or with only one hand. He must keep the lifts looking easy and light and lower the girl softly and carefully to the floor.

Every jump must begin, as in solo dance, with a demi-plié or fondu. He must lightly but firmly place his hands on her body as if to help her with her demi-plié as he simultaneously bends his knees when the girl bends hers. He must remember to lift her UPWARDS ONLY and never to push her forwards away from himself, and at the same time, he must NEVER push his own weight backwards.

After a jump with a change of feet, the girl should make a slight change of épaulement as she would in solo dance. The boy must coordinate his movement with this slight change in her shoulders in order to help the girl move into the correct direction and pose as she lands.

During any temps levé sauté, the boy must understand how to carry the girl forwards, sideways, or backwards during the jump, NOT when it begins.

During sissonnes fermées, pas ballonnés and other traveling movements that go forward, sideways or backwards, the boy must travel with the girl and lower her softly to the floor, holding a position after each jump. When holding the girl during pas ballonnés, the boy should not, as a rule, be behind the girl, but should be just to her left or right side.

Principle for the Support of Small Jumps with Two Hands at the Waist

Before the start of the lift, the boy presses the girl's waist with his hands as if forcing her into the demi-plié which they do together. The boy must lift upwards, neither pushing the girl forwards away from himself nor pulling her towards himself.

Lift in Changement de Pied

The girl stands in Fifth Position, right foot devant, her arms in Preparatory Position. The boy stands behind her in Second Position, with both hands on her waist. The boy signals the preparation for the jump and as both partners demi-plié, the boy shifts his palms downward so that his fingers are pointing upwards. The girl does a changement de pied, and as the jump reaches its crest, the boy straightens up for the lift, his hands at chest level. (Sketch 55. Crest of the lift in changement de pied.)

The boy then softly lowers the girl to the floor into demi-plié. The position of the girl's épaulement at the end of the jump is changed with the help of the boy, who turns the girl's body in the desired direction. The boy's back must be kept straight during the lift, and the hand position should be carefully mastered since it is the position for the majority of lifts with support at the waist.

55. The crest of the lift in changement de pied

Lift in Pas Assemblé with Support by Both Hands at the Waist

The girl begins in Fifth Position, right foot derrière, arms in Preparatory Position. The boy stands behind her, slightly to the right of the girl's right shoulder. Both of his hands are on her waist. (Sketch 56a. Preparation for pas assemblé lift.) Together, they do a glissade along a diagonal to corner 2 (Sketch 56b. The partners in glissade together), ending in demi-plié. After the boy has shifted his palms as described in the previous lift, the girl does a pas assemblé and the boy lifts her, carrying her slightly in the direction of corner 2. (Sketch 56c. Crest of the lift in pas assemblé with correct écarté position.) The boy then softly lowers her into a balanced Fifth Position in demi-plié. The boy must strictly preserve the écarté position during the assemblé.

56a. Preparation for pas
assemblé lift

56b. The partners in
glissade together

56c. Crest of the lift in pas assemblé with correct écarté position

Lift from Sissonne Ending in First Arabesque

The girl begins in Fifth Position, right foot devant, with her arms in First Position. The boy stands behind her, hands at her waist. (Sketch 57a. Preparation for a lift in First Arabesque.) After he signals, they both demi-plié and the boy moves his hands along her beltline. At the same time, he shifts his palms downwards so his fingers are slightly upwards and shifts his left hand just behind, and a little higher towards, the girl's left shoulder blade, fingers upwards. This shifting of hands stabilizes the proper position of the First Arabesque and makes the lift comfortable. At the crest of the jump, he lifts the girl and steps onto the right foot. He then softly lowers her to the floor still in First Arabesque on the right pointe. (Sketch 57b. Crest of the lift in First Arabesque with correctly shifted palms.) The arabesque may end directly where it started or a small or large distance to the right.

57a. Preparation for a lift
in First Arabesque

57b. Crest of the lift in First Arabesque
with correctly shifted palms

In temps levés sautés, pas de chat, pas de basque, and other small movements, the boy must practice carrying the girl forwards, to the side, and backwards. In sissonne fermé, pas ballonné, and larger jumps, he usually begins to the right or left of the girl. The shift of hands precedes lifts in grand jeté, soubresaut, cabriole, and First, Second, Third, and Fourth Arabesques, as well as in other poses.

Serebrennikov gives a word of warning: "Correct placement of the palms is essential. Placing palms on the hip bone or waist is not uncomfortable for the girl unless the fingers press into the rib cage, which can be painful. In the beginning, the lifts should not be high since it is more important to increase the duration of the jump, and most importantly, the boy must strive for lightness and ease, and must soften to the UTMOST the descent of the girl into a balanced position on the floor."

9 · Point of Support for Aerial Partnering

SEREBRENNIKOV continues with larger and more difficult lifts and advises the boys to take advantage of gymnastic or weight-lifting work.

He reminds us that all jumps are preceded by demi-pliés and that they are performed by the girl after an unnoticeable signal by the boy before the jump.

Grand Assemblé with Support by One Hand, the Other at the Waist

The girl stands on her right foot in First Arabesque par terre, facing corner 2. The boy, at the distance of one step behind her, holds her left hand from below with his left hand palm-to-palm, right arm in Third Position. His pose is an easy First Arabesque par terre. (Sketch 57c. Starting pose for grand assemblé from corner 2 to corner 6.) The girl does pas chassé tombé backwards, stepping onto her left foot toward corner 6, jumps straight up into grand assemblé, and finishes in the air in écarté to corner 6.

As the girl does pas chassé, the boy puts his right hand on her LEFT side, fingers upward, and moves along with the pas chassé; after this he takes a big step forward

57c. Starting pose for grand assemblé from corner 2 to corner 6

onto his left foot, and with a half turn, finishes
the movement with a big thrust upwards and
lunges onto his right foot. As the girl jumps
into the grand assemblé, he straightens his
right elbow and pushes the girl, now flying
through the air, away from himself as
if tightening a bowstring. (Sketch 57d.
Position at the crest of the jump
for grand assemblé.) He softens
her landing.

57d. Position at the crest of the jump for
grand assemblé

Grand Assemblé around the Boy with Support by Two Hands

The starting pose is the same as in the previous exercise. The girl then turns to
face the boy and raises her right arm into Third Position, palm toward the boy.
He takes her hand with his right hand, palm-to-palm, their left hands in First
Position. (Sketch 58a. Preparation for grand assemblé around the boy.) After
sissonne tombé onto the left foot, the girl does grand assemblé, as above, with
the right leg passing behind the boy at the crest of the jump in écarté behind
him toward point 3.

At the moment the girl pushes away from the floor, the boy sharply stretches
both his arms as he lifts the girl upwards and circles his arm around his head,
leaning slightly forward as the girl flies behind him as closely as possible.
(Sketch 58b. Crest of the jump in grand assemblé around the boy.) A suggested
ending, after landing in Fifth Position right foot devant, is a tour soutenu to the
left aided by the boy. Various approaches such as pas chassé and pas de bourrée
are given at a distance of three or four paces before the strong pas tombé with
palm-to-palm contact.

58b. Crest of the jump in grand assemblé around the boy

58a. Preparation for grand assemblé around the boy

Jeté Entrelacé with Support by One Hand, the Other on the Hip

The starting pose is the same as above for both partners. The girl does a pas chassé tombé and then steps onto the left leg and does jeté entrelacé on a diagonal line from corner 2 to corner 6. As she does the pas chassé, the boy supports her with his right hand on her hip, fingers pointing downward. Both the boy's and the girl's left arms are in First Position. At the crest of the jump, the boy lifts the girl with his right arm as high as possible while his left hand gives support to the girl's left arm. (Sketch 59. Crest of the movement in jeté entrelacé.) The boy must strongly hold both arms in this position to lower the girl softly. The jeté entrelacé may finish in Second Arabesque or attitude effacée.

59. Crest of the movement in jeté entrelacé

Change from Attitude Effacée into a Horizontal Position with Support by One Arm around the Waist and One over the Body at the Thigh

The girl stands in attitude effacée on her left pointe, her left arm around the boy's shoulder. The boy faces point 1, on the left side of the girl, his right arm cradling her around the waist, his fingertips on her right hip, left arm in Second Position, and his left leg in a lunge toward corner 8. (Sketch 60a. Starting pose for change from attitude effacée into horizontal pose.) The girl descends from pointe into fondu and with her right leg does a grand battement jeté toward point 7 with a strong jump, placing her body in a horizontal position with her back to the floor. At the same time, she must pull her left leg quickly behind her right leg into Fifth Position. At the moment the girl does her battement jeté, the boy throws the girl up with his right arm as he slips it further around her waist and cradles over to her right side, his left hand holding her thighs just above the knees.

While changing into the horizontal position, the girl must avoid making a break in her body or a right angle where the trunk and legs join and must fix her vertical position immovably. As she throws her leg into the air, she leans backwards and raises her arms into Third Position. (Sketch 60b. Completed movement in horizontal pose.) Notice that the boy has changed into a lunge onto the right leg toward point 3.

Using both arms, the boy lifts the girl upwards from the horizontal position to a vertical Fifth Position, his left foot in a lunge as he shifts his center of gravity back to the left leg and turns the girl to finish with her back to point 7, as he lowers her to the floor in Fifth Position sur les pointes at the outer side of his left foot. (Sketch 60c. Final pose from horizontal position.)

Development of the muscles of the upper back and arms is important for girls, and some gymnastic work to strengthen these areas would be an asset.

Pas Sissonne in First Arabesque with Support by One Hand

Both the girl and boy behind her stand in Fifth Position, right foot devant, arms in Preparatory Position. Together, they do pas sissonne tombé onto the right foot, and the girl alone does pas sissonne in First Arabesque. At the same mo-

60a. Starting pose
for change from
attitude effacée into
horizontal pose

60c. Final pose from
horizontal position

60b. Completed move-
ment in horizontal pose

ment, the boy supports her with his right hand on her right wrist. The girl then does failli and pas assemblé ending in Fifth Position right foot devant, or she may end the movement in another way. This support in First Arabesque is frequently used as an ending movement as partners go to another place onstage, or it may be used as an exit from stage.

Grand Fouetté Sauté with Support by One Hand

The girl stands on her left pointe in First Arabesque or à terre facing corner 8. (Sketch 61a. Starting pose for grand fouetté sauté with support by one hand.) The boy stands behind her at the distance of one step in arabesque par terre and holds her right hand with his right hand, palm-to-palm. He then pulls her slightly by the hand toward him as she does a pas chassé backwards along a diagonal to corner 4. Then, facing corner 4, she steps onto the right leg, throws the left leg high into fouetté sauté, ends in attitude croisée, and relevés onto pointe. (Sketch 61b. Final pose in attitude croisée from grand fouetté.)

61a. Starting pose for grand fouetté sauté with support by one hand

61b. Final pose in attitude croisée from grand fouetté

At the crest of the jump, the girl pushes against the boy's hand which has now moved to Second Position in order to increase the height of her jump without changing her right arm in First Position. He ends in a lunge on the left leg toward corner 8.

A Small Lift from Falling Position

The boy stands behind the girl who is in Fifth Position, right foot devant, arms in Third Position. The boy grasps the girl around the waist with his right arm and places his left hand around and over her body to the left thigh, lifting her into the horizontal position as he lunges onto the right leg as in Sketch 6ob. He recovers the girl's fall by shifting from the right leg to an upright position as he places the girl on both feet as in Sketch 6oc.

Small Lift from First Arabesque into Fish Pose

The girl stands in First Arabesque on her right pointe. The boy stands behind her, both hands on her waist. As he lunges into Fourth Position onto the right leg, he cradles under the girl's waist with his right hand, turning his fingers upward (palm on the hip bone) and placing his left hand around the center of her left thigh, just above his own left hip. (Sketch 62. Preparatory position from First Arabesque into fish pose.) Then, straightening himself up onto both legs, he lifts the girl and shifts his center of gravity to the right leg with the left leg in battement tendu position to point 7. At the moment of the lift, the girl moves the pointe of her right foot to the mid-section of her left shin. During the lift, the boy must not disturb her pose NOR LEAN FORWARD AS HE LIFTS. In the lifted pose, the girl softly bends her upper back and head backwards. (Sketch 63. Crest of the lift in fish pose.)

To return to First Arabesque, the boy shifts his center of gravity still more to the right leg, slightly lifting the girl as she straightens her right leg to support the arabesque on pointe. The boy then returns to his demi-plié position on the right leg as he changes his hands to her waist, first the left hand and then the right.

62. Preparatory position from First Arabesque into fish pose

63. Crest of the lift
in small fish pose

Small Lift from First Arabesque into Swallow Pose

From the previous fish pose, the boy, instead of placing the girl into First Arabesque, lifts and lowers the girl onto his left thigh after he shifts his demi-plié onto the left leg and stretches out his right leg to corner 2. As the girl is lowered onto the boy's thigh, she forcibly bends both knees together into her swallow pose, with her feet lightly touching his left shoulder blade. As soon as the boy feels the placement of her feet on his shoulder, he leans backwards and supports the girl by balancing her on his thigh. At first the boy may want to hold the girl at the waist, then open his left arm to the side and the right arm slightly forward. (Sketch 64. Final swallow pose from fish pose.)

For the return, the boy must cradle his right hand under the girl's waist and his left arm on her left thigh. As she straightens both legs, he replaces her on the floor in First Arabesque.

64. Final swallow pose from fish pose

First Arabesque with Step onto Boy's Thigh

The girl stands in corner 4 on her left foot, right pointe tendue devant, left arm in First Position, right arm in Second Position, palms down. The boy is in front of the girl at the distance of about 2 steps, down on his left knee, or in a lunge, his right knee toward corner 2, right arm in Third Position and left arm in Second Position, palm down. HIS RIGHT HIP JOINT MUST FORM A SHARP RIGHT ANGLE and be perpendicular to the diagonal between corners 2 and 6. The girl steps onto her right foot, then places her left foot on the boy's right thigh, DIRECTLY AGAINST HIS BODY, and straightens up into First Arabesque. He supports her with his right hand on her waist at the small of her back and with the left hand under her rib cage. Or the boy may support her with both hands. (Sketch 65. First Arabesque on boy's thigh with two-hand support. Final poses.)

The girl may approach this First Arabesque by jumping from pas couru or from pas glissade. The boy remains in a deep lunge so that his thigh and trunk form a right angle. She may stand without hand support. Or she may descend from the arabesque by first making a passé into pose effacée with her right leg and then falling onto her right foot toward corner 2 into First or Second Arabesque. The boy softens her landing by holding her at the waist and circling her body with his right arm to the mid-section of the right thigh as in the fish pose. He puts her onto the floor in First Arabesque as he straightens up.

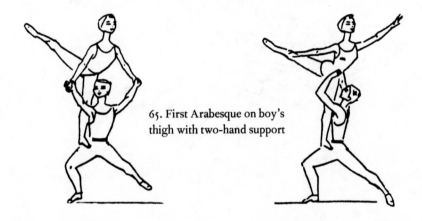

65. First Arabesque on boy's thigh with two-hand support

Fish Pose from Sitting Position with Support from One Hand

The girl sits on the floor facing corner 2, knees bent and together, feet on the floor. The boy stands in front of her at the distance of 2 steps in a free and arbitrary pose. He then lunges onto his left leg towards the girl and stretches his right arm toward her, palm up. She places her right hand SECURELY in his, palm down, or may use a wrist grip. The boy pulls hard from the shoulder bringing the girl toward him as she pushes herself up and away from the floor, first with her left foot, then from her right. THIS MUST BE A VERY STRONG PUSH AWAY FROM THE FLOOR. She lets go of the boy's hand in the air and takes the pose of the fish as the boy grasps her with his right arm cradled around her waist, his left arm at the mid-section of her left thigh. (Sketch 66. Final fish pose from floor jump.) His pull is preceded by a hardly noticeable signal which is a push in the OPPOSITE direction to the direction of the jump (as in the shifting of hands in the direction opposite a turn), and like all signals, it occurs before the count or beat.

The girl must not begin the jump independently. Neither must she bend her wrist during the lift to fish pose, nor tighten her arm, nor bend the elbow of the pulled arm before the movement.

As a variation, the girl may also turn in the air during the jump so that she lands in a horizontal position with her back to the floor.

66. Final fish pose
from floor jump

10 · Aerial Lifts to Chest Level

As THE aerial portion of pas de deux dance becomes more complicated and difficult, Serebrennikov again mentions the need for a spotter, a person who stands nearby during the exercises of turns and lifts in the air to catch the girl should the boy misjudge his tempo or the placement of the lift or jump. He stresses the importance of placing a lift correctly, and reminds us that the explanation for the exercise should be given to the girl first, then to the boy, and should be executed separately, and, in the presence of the spotter, mastered in sequence.

Principle for Incomplete or Complete Turns in the Air
from a Horizontal Position

In turns that begin from a horizontal position, the boy must always throw the girl's turn TOWARD himself and never away from himself.

In this exercise, the boy does demi-plié in Second Position and supports the girl in a cradle hold with his right arm, his left arm over her body and around her thigh. As he straightens up, he throws the girl upwards and toward himself for an incomplete or complete turn, catching her in the previous arm positions, again in demi-plié.

Support with Two Hands of an Incomplete Turn
from a Horizontal Position Beginning in First Arabesque

The girl stands on her right pointe in First Arabesque, facing point 3. The boy, directly behind her, in Second Position, bends his knees slightly. Both his hands are on her waist. After a signal, she does a demi-plié on the right leg as he lifts and throws her toward himself. At the crest of the jump, and in one sharp movement, she straightens her right leg into Fifth Position in front of her raised left leg, raises her arms into Third Position, and makes a full turn to the left toward the boy, ending with her back to the floor. The boy must catch her with his right arm underneath her waist, left arm over the body and around her right thigh, as he softens the catch by returning to a demi-plié after straightening up for the toss and turn.

This exercise may also begin from a horizontal position, back to the floor. (Sketch 67. Horizontal position, back to the floor.) The ending then may be in First Arabesque. The spotter may stand in front of the partners during this exercise, ready to prevent injury or a fall to the floor. The spotter's back should be to point 1 and his hands well below the girl's body to provide a net. The spotter must pay particular attention to protecting the girl's head should she begin to slip to the floor.

67. Horizontal position, back to floor

For Support with Two Hands for a Jump into a Horizontal Position from Pas Glissade

The girl stands on her left foot, back to point 3, right leg in pose croisée tendue à terre forward toward point 7. The boy may stand in any given pose, facing point 1 at three or four paces from the girl in a direct line from her position, point 3 to 7. The girl does a pas glissade toward the boy and pushes strongly from the floor with the left leg, throwing her body into a horizontal position. Her arms change to Third Position at the crest of the jump. (Sketch 68. Crest of the jump from pas glissade.) In changing into this horizontal pose, the girl must pay particular attention to the correctness of her body by not bending backwards nor holding the position too loosely. Her body must not "corner" by forming a sharp angle at the point where the hipbone and thigh meet. At the moment the girl does the pas glissade, the boy lunges onto his right foot, leans his body in the direction of the girl's flight, and catches her with his right arm cradling around her waist and his left arm over her body to her right thigh.

The exercise may begin from pas de bourrée or pas couru. The spotter stands in the same position as in the previous exercise.

68. Crest of jump from pas glissade

Support by Two Hands after Jeté Entrelacé Finishing in Fish Pose

The girl stands in First Arabesque par terre on the right leg facing corner 2. The boy stands in any given pose, at a distance of two or three paces, on a DIAGONAL line from corner 2 to corner 6. The girl does pas chassé tombé on her left foot followed by a jeté entrelacé along a diagonal line from corner 2 to corner 6. At the crest of the jump, the girl assumes the fish pose in which she will land in the boy's arms.

At the moment of the jeté entrelacé, the boy transfers his center line of balance onto his right foot and stretches his right arm forwards, and, turning the palm of his hand upwards, catches the girl so that the tips of his fingers are on the left side of her pelvis. With his left hand, he holds her left thigh. His left arm passes over her body and grasps her left thigh at the finish of the fish pose. The girl must jump exactly in front of the boy. Exactness in execution of the pas will assure lightness and clarity.

Jump into Boy's Arms Ending in a Horizontal Position

Begin this movement as in the previous exercise with a jump into horizontal position from pas glissade. The girl stands on her LEFT leg with her back to point 3 in pose croisée devant à terre. The boy stands facing point 1, three or four paces from the girl, in a direct line from point 3 to point 7. The girl does a pas glissade, posé right and throws her left leg forcefully upwards. At the time of the girl's glissade, the boy lunges onto his right foot, inclining his body toward her and moving his left hand over her right thigh to cradle his right arm under her waist. During the first attempts, the girl may curve her left arm around the boy's shoulders, embracing his neck for support.

The jump should be studied from various preparations such as pas de bourrée and pas couru. The girl must not fly past the boy but calculate the size and distance of her jump.

Grand Fouetté Sauté Ending in Fish Pose

The preparation is the same as in the previous exercise. The girl does pas glissade, posé right, and throws her left leg toward point 7 in grand fouetté sauté, ending in First Arabesque facing point 3. The boy catches her in the air with his right arm under her body and his left arm over her body to her left thigh. She assumes the fish pose during the descent of the jump, taking care to keep her back to the boy during her flight.
(Sketch 69. Crest of the jump from grand fouetté sauté.)
At the end of the jump, the girl's shoulder blades must be strongly pressed to the boy's chest.

69. Crest of jump from grand fouetté sauté

Support by One Hand Around the Waist During Grand Jeté with Stabilization of the Pose in Flight

The girl stands in the farthest corner of the stage, back to corner 4, on her left foot, pose croisée devant à terre. The boy stands in any given pose, in the center of the stage facing the girl, at a distance of four or five paces. The girl does pas couru and then a grand jeté en attitude to corner 8, placing the crest of the jump directly in front of the boy. At the moment the girl does pas couru, the boy lunges forward and stretches his right arm forward, guiding the girl's jump. He catches the girl in flight (at the crest of the jump) around the back of the waist while his left arm remains in Second Position. At the crest of the jump, the girl circles the boy's neck with her left arm and supports herself by strongly pressing her arm down on his shoulders. (Sketch 70. Crest and landing of the jump in grand jeté.) He turns to the left three or four times, stabilizing the pose as he moves to corner 8. The exercise ends in Second Arabesque fondue, after the boy softens the girl's descent by lightly guiding her to the floor with his left hand.

Serebrennikov gives an effective alternative ending: During the last turn, the girl may use the momentum of the turn to swing her right leg into Fifth Position over her left leg. (Sketch 71a. Swing to Fifth during turns following grand jeté.) She ends sitting on the boy's left thigh. (Sketch 71b. Final pose after swing to Fifth Position.)

70. Crest and landing of jump in grand jeté

71a. Swing to Fifth during
turns following grand jeté

71b. Final pose after swing
to Fifth Position

Support by Two Hands for a Fish Pose from a Running Jump

The girl begins at the farthest end of the stage, back to corner 6, in a given pose. The boy stands in the center of the stage in any given pose, facing the girl at a distance of five or six paces. The girl starts to run toward corner 2, does petit assemblé right foot, strongly pushing off from both feet, and flies toward the boy. She assumes the fish pose during the flight. (Sketch 72a. Flight into fish pose from a running start.) The jump should be as high as the boy's shoulders.

At the crest of the jump, the boy lunges onto his left leg, stretches out his right arm forwards and catches the girl in a cradle hold around the front of her waist, his left arm over her body to catch her left thigh. (Sketch 72b. Final pose

72a. Flight into fish pose from a running start

72b. Final pose from running start

from running start.) After catching the girl, the boy shifts his center of gravity from his left leg to the right leg and softens the descent of the jump.

At the beginning of this study, the jump is made from both feet as in pas assemblé or from one foot as in pas sissonne. The spotter stands facing the boy, back to point 1, with his left arm well below the girl's body during the flight to act as a net.

After mastering this jump, the girl may perform it ending in a horizontal position, back to the floor. The girl, as she jumps, makes a full turn to the left, the boy catching her with his right arm under her waist and his left on her right thigh. This jump is seldom performed on the opposite side. The boy must always be careful how he transfers his weight from his left to his right leg and be certain that his body follows the line of the girl's flight downwards.

At this point, Serebrennikov gives the principles for higher jumps and for poses that rest on the chest or shoulder. With these lifts come new principles. The girl must be in a firm pose on the boy's chest or shoulders. Both partners must acquire the habit of holding absolutely still and erect, whether moving in a circle or turning en place three or more times.

Support by Two Hands for a Lift to the Chest in a Sitting Pose

The girl stands in Fifth Position, right foot devant, arms in Preparatory Position. The boy is behind her, hands on her waist. The girl rises sur les pointes, holding her position and opening her arms sideways; she then gently bends both knees into demi-plié and pushes off into the jump. At the same time as the jump, she raises her arms to Third Position. (Later, the arms can be varied as decided by the teacher.)

The boy coordinates his demi-plié with that of the girl, and as she jumps he must lift her strongly. Taking a half step forwards, he places her on his chest, changing his arms and elbows so that they are gripping her thighs with the palms of his hands holding the front part of her waist. She may then open her right leg at 90 degrees (croisé), with the left leg slightly bent at the knee and pressed firmly against the boy's right side. (Sketch 73a. Front view sitting on the partner's chest; 73b. Side view.) THE GIRL MUST NEVER LOOK DOWN.

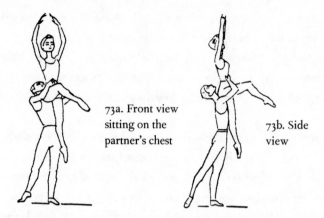

73a. Front view sitting on the partner's chest

73b. Side view

The boy must replace his hands on the girl's waist before he softly lowers her to the floor. She must straighten her body and, with both legs slightly forward, slide down the boy's chest returning to the floor on one or two feet.

If the girl is wearing a tunic or very full skirt, he must not squeeze his fingers or elbows in such a way as to destroy the line of her costume when he lifts her to his chest or shoulder.

Support with Two Hands for a Lift to the Shoulder Ending in a Sitting Pose

The principle for lifting the girl onto the shoulder is the same as above. Before the lift to the right shoulder, the boy's hands are usually placed to the right so that his left hand is a little more forward and upward on the girl's left side when the lift takes place. If the lift is on the left shoulder, then the left hand is on the waist and the right a little higher on her right side.

This exercise begins as the previous one for a lift to the chest. As the girl jumps, the boy lifts her upwards with both hands, at the same time taking a small step forwards onto his left foot and placing her onto his right shoulder. The boy must lift the girl high enough to be slightly above his shoulder so that she may sit correctly. The boy keeps his right arm cradled around her waist, fingers reaching toward the right thigh. His left hand is directed toward her left hip. Her left arm rises to Third Position, right to Second.

He lowers her softly keeping two hands on her waist. (Sketch 74. Sitting pose on the partner's shoulder.) Once the lift has been mastered, the boy may hold the girl with his right arm only and open his left into Second Position.

Support with Two Hands at the Waist in a Lift to the Shoulder Sitting in Attitude Allongée

This exercise begins in the same manner as the previous exercise for a lift to the shoulder ending in a sitting pose after the girl reaches the crest of the jump. At that moment, the boy places his right shoulder underneath the girl by taking a small step forward. His right hand stays at the right side of her waist, and the left hand moves front to the center of her waist. The boy leans his head slightly to the left and presses her tightly to him as she sits on his right shoulder on her left thigh. Immediately upon sitting, the girl takes an attitude allongée pose by bending her left knee slightly, not turned out, and touching her right knee with it in attitude allongée behind her. Her arms are in a given pose with her back kept strictly straight throughout the lift as it should be in all lifts. (Sketch 75. Lift to attitude allongée on the shoulder.)

When the boy feels secure with this lift, he may support her with his right hand alone and open his left arm into Second Position. The transition from the crest of the jump to the attitude allongée is a difficult one and requires a spotter to stand in front of the girl until the movement is mastered.

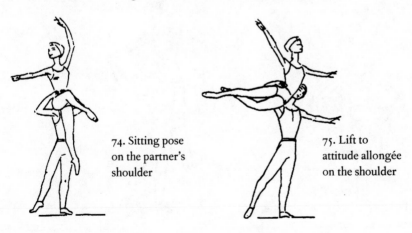

74. Sitting pose on the partner's shoulder

75. Lift to attitude allongée on the shoulder

Support by Two Hands to Two Hands for a Lift to the Shoulder Ending in a Croisé Sitting Pose

The girl stands on right pointe, left retiré croisé devant and toward point 3. Her right arm is in First Position, palm down; her left arm is in Second Position, the back of her hand directed towards point 1. With the palm of his right hand upwards, the boy holds the girl's right wrist firmly. Her left hand is in the boy's left, palms together. His left elbow is bent.

The boy kneels on his right knee as near to the girl's right point as possible, but without changing the relationship of his shoulders to point 1, and places his right shoulder under her left thigh. She sits on his shoulder. Her spine must be absolutely straight as he rises, both arms fully stretched and held strongly, but with her head slightly turned and inclined to the left. His left elbow is bent. (Sketch 76a. Preparation for lift ending in pose croisée.)

The girl's spine must remain vertical throughout the lift to and descent from the boy's shoulder as both her arms straighten out at the elbow. The lift is performed WITHOUT DEMI-PLIÉ and depends entirely upon the strength of the boy's legs as he straightens up, keeping his body absolutely erect. (Sketch 76b. Final pose.)

The girl is returned to the floor in one of two ways. The boy may descend to his right knee into the original starting position, keeping his back straight until

76a. Preparation for lift ending in pose croisée

76b. Final pose

the girl is once again on her right pointe. Or the boy may lunge toward point 3 and bend his body slightly to the right as the girl slides from his shoulder or jumps to the floor into Fifth Position in demi-plié.

Support with Two Hands for a Lift in Horizontal Position One Underneath the Thigh

The girl stands in Fifth Position sur les pointes, left foot devant, arms in Third Position. The boy kneels on his right knee behind her, his right arm curved around behind her body, his left in Second Position. The girl falls backwards, placing the back of her waist on his right shoulder. The boy straightens up with both legs and lifts the girl upwards. He places his left hand under her left thigh and directs her feet to the correct point. He must be steady upon rising and keep his body vertical throughout the movement. (Sketch 77. Final pose of lift to shoulder in horizontal position.)

This position may also be reached from the fish pose. From the fish pose, the boy straightens up from his kneeling position and swings the girl with both hands onto his shoulder into the horizontal position.

77. Final pose of lift to shoulder in horizontal position

Support by Two Hands to Two Hands for a Kneel on the Shoulder, Ending in Arabesque

The girl faces point 1 in a given pose with the boy kneeling on his right knee, left knee toward point 7, at the right side of the girl. He offers his right hand palm up. The girl places her right hand on his overhead right hand, palm down, and her left hand on his left hand, palm down. She then places her left foot on the boy's left thigh directly against his body. She presses down on his hands as she raises her right knee and kneels on his right shoulder as she opens her left leg backwards into First Arabesque. (Sketch 78a. Preparation for step on boy's thigh into arabesque on shoulder; Sketch 78b. Final pose with knee on shoulder.)

After the girl's knee is placed upon his shoulder, the boy stands up, keeping his back straight, facing corner 2, elbows straight and lifted to support the arabesque. The boy must begin to turn to corner 2 before the girl raises and places her knee on his shoulder.

The return to the floor varies but is most frequently performed as a lunge by the boy onto the right leg as the girl lowers her left and stretches her right leg into Third Arabesque as her left toe reaches the floor.

Lastly, Serebrennikov adds: "In stage work, when one meets situations where the girl stands on the boy's shoulder in whatever pose, the boy supports her with both hands at the waist. He must learn to move carrying her in a straight line or circle and while making one or more turns."

78a. Preparation for step on boy's thigh into arabesque on shoulder

78b. Final pose with knee on shoulder

11 · Aerial Lifts to Shoulder Level

AS WE BEGIN the last chapters of Serebrennikov's textbook on pas de deux dance, it is important to remember that we are also nearing the end of the four-year study of pas de deux within the eight-year study at the Vaganova Ballet Academy. During this period, the students have become stronger in technique, and hopefully, have mastered all the previous exercises of pas terre and aerial partnering.

Although Serebrennikov points out at the beginning of the study that students might be unequal in technique and size, it is now important that the partners be more equally matched and that a spotter be present at all times. The teacher must stop the practice at any sign of fatigue. It will also become apparent at this point that only a few partners will be able to accomplish the complicated and exciting lifts of the last chapters. But this chapter should be well within the capability of the professional dancer.

Serebrennikov continues to emphasize that these movements should evolve tastefully from the choreography and should not be used for pyrotechnic display.

In these last chapters, the girl, no matter how slight her build nor fearless her spirit, should not attempt these lifts until she has developed a clear and strong demi-plié and jump; a strong arch in the upper back; a good sense of "common tempo" with her partner; good judgment in the placement of her body in a lift in relation to the boy; strong muscles in her arms to aid her in supporting herself; and most of all, a calm manner during precarious moments to allow her partner and the spotter to correct a lift or facilitate a return to the floor.

The boy, by the same token, must now learn additional positions of support at the waist, mid-thigh, and ilium (the largest of the three bones composing either lateral half of the pelvis at the spine). The new points of support are the hip bones; the placement of the palm at the middle of the front of the waist with fingers facing upwards toward the sternum; the bent knee; under the arm; and the "sit" bones. Hopefully, from his work in gymnastics or dance therapy classes, the boy has developed shoulder and arm muscles from his weight-lifting exercises and knows the importance of lifting from a deep demi-plié with a straight back. He must now learn to lift directly overhead with locked shoulder and elbow position and how to soften a descent by lowering the girl's weight to his chest and then to the floor.

Finding the Support for Aerial Lifts to Shoulder Level

1. The first three examples of big jumps to the shoulder ending in fish or swallow poses begin in the floor position described earlier. The descents are as given in the earlier exercises.

   The girl stands in Fifth Position, right foot devant in effacé position facing corner 2. From there, she bends her knees and lowers herself onto her left knee and continues the movement downwards until she is sitting on the floor with her right leg straight out toward corner 2. Her right arm is in First Position, her left arm is in Second Position, both palms down. The left shoulder is now turned slightly toward corner 8 and there is a lean backwards. The boy, who is in a deep lunge toward corner 6, offers his right hand to the girl with a gracious gesture. She lowers her right hand onto his hand. He gives a light and almost invisible pull as a signal and the girl quickly pushes off the floor from her right foot. During her jump, she makes a half-turn to the left with such precision that her buttocks land on the boy's shoulder. Her body must be stretched into the horizontal position, her arms in Third, her legs stretched outwards in Fifth, with right foot devant. (Sketch 79. Lying horizontally on the partner's shoulder.) The boy guides and then holds her on his right shoulder and immediately cradles his right arm around her waist and places his left hand under her left thigh. At the moment when the girl lands on the boy's shoulder, his legs must spring up to

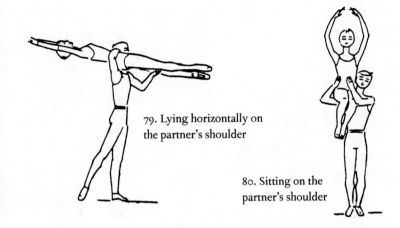

79. Lying horizontally on the partner's shoulder

80. Sitting on the partner's shoulder

withstand the strength of her jump and the weight of her body. He can then direct the line of her pose to any point decided by the teacher. The girl must remain still, straight, and NEVER GIVE IN AT THE WAIST.

2. The boy helps the girl to spring into the air as in the previous exercise. She turns toward the boy to the right during the jump and sits on his right shoulder. Her arms are raised in Third Position, legs bent at the knee in Sixth Position (not turned-out). The girl's body and both hips and knees must all face the same direction. The boy's right arm holds her right side. His left is in front of her left side, fingers upwards, and he turns to face point 1, straightening his knees. (Sketch 80. Sitting on the partner's shoulder.)

3. The girl jumps onto the boy's shoulder, finishing in a swallow pose. (Sketch 81a. Crest of the jump to partner's shoulder; 81b. Ending in swallow pose.) To perform this lift from the floor, the girl must push off strongly with her right foot as the boy pulls her right arm with his right. The girl takes the in-flight swallow pose as the boy immediately puts his left arm around her waist and takes her right wrist in his right hand, bringing her to rest on his left shoulder. He must make a turn clockwise so that she will finish in swallow pose completely stabilized with the boy facing point 1. He can then place his right hand just above the right side of her waist and take two or three steps forward in the direction of the jump, which gives the audience the illusion of a greater, longer flight.

81a. Crest of the jump to partner's shoulder   81b. Ending in swallow pose

Big Jump to the Boy's Shoulder, Finishing in Sitting Position, Using a Two-hand Hold

The girl stands with her back to corner 8 on her right foot in pose croisée à terre. Her left arm is in Third, palm toward the boy, her right in First, palm down. The boy faces the girl on his left foot, right stretched backwards, arms in the same position as the girl's. He takes her right hand in his right and her left in his left, palms facing palms. (Sketch 82a. Preparation for jump to the shoulder with two-hand support.) The girl does pas couru with the left foot towards the boy's spine and pushes off with the right foot from the floor. She must jump strongly and press herself upwards on his hands. During the jump, she bends her left knee and raises it to 90 degrees (not turned-out). She must calculate and control the jump in such a way that her left buttock rests on the boy's right shoulder in the sitting position. As the girl jumps, she must pass directly behind the boy's spine as at the same moment with a swift movement, he catches her and lifts his arms upwards. Only when she is firmly sitting on his shoulder must he fully lunge onto the right leg or fully stretch his legs. (Sketch 82b. Final pose on shoulder.) The return to the floor is accomplished as in previous exercises.

82a. Preparation for jump to
shoulder with two-hand support

82b. Final pose on shoulder

Big Jump Finishing with a Knee on the Boy's Shoulder

The preparation is the same as in the previous exercise except that the boy does
not turn, but brings his right foot forward. The girl steps onto her left foot,
does a glissade, forcibly pushes off with her left foot from the floor behind the
boy's spine, and jumps onto his right shoulder by bending her right knee and
stretching the left downward behind the boy. The descent is the same as in the
previous exercises. Note that the vertical positions must be held by both the boy
and girl throughout all the movements.

Jeté Entrelacé to the Boy's Shoulder with Two-hand Hold

The girl stands with her back to corner 2 on her right foot, left pointe tendue
devant. Her right arm is in Third, palm toward the boy, her left in First, palm
down. The boy faces her on his right foot, left stretched backward. His arms
are in the same position as hers. He takes her hands in his, palm to palm. (Sketch
83a. Preparation for the jump in jeté entrelacé in a diagonal toward corner 6.)
With a step onto her left foot, the girl does jeté entrelacé in a diagonal towards

83a. Preparation for the jump in jeté entrelacé in a diagonal towards corner 6

83b. Final pose on boy's shoulder

corner 6, aiming at resting the center of her right thigh exactly on the boy's left shoulder, leaning her body lightly against his neck. She then brings her left leg toward her right very swiftly and balances in the swallow pose. When making this jump, the girl must not fly past the boy, otherwise she will land on his shoulder uncomfortably on her waist or stomach, not on her pelvis.

As the girl jumps, the boy must bend slightly without thrusting his left shoulder backward and give a sharp pull and thrust of his arms upward and very slightly forward, raising them fully only when he feels that the girl is firmly fixed on his shoulder. He must continue to hold her firmly with both hands and keep his spine absolutely straight. (Sketch 83b. Final pose on boy's shoulder.)

For the girl's descent to the floor, the boy kneels on his right knee. She lowers first one leg and then the other to stand on the floor in Fifth Position behind him. If the girl has alighted on the boy's right shoulder, he should kneel on the left knee.

The jump onto the shoulder from jeté entrelacé should be studied using one hand only. More advanced students should practice taking the pose from various other poses and preparations. If the girl begins the jump from a run, or both boy and girl move around each other, their hands should join just before the jump so that the pull from the boy's arm and the push of the girl's foot from the floor are given greater impetus.

Jeté Entrelacé to the Boy's Shoulder with One Hand on the Hip, the Other Around the Waist

The preparation is the same as in the previous exercise, but the boy does not hold the girl's hands. He stands facing her about two steps away. The girl does pas chassé; left foot does a sharp tombé into jeté entrelacé toward corner 6 and onto the boy's left shoulder. As the girl does pas chassé, the boy stretches his right arm forward, fingers upward, and holds her at the middle of her waist. As she brushes her right foot upward, he catches her by curving his right arm below both her thighs and without thrusting his left shoulder backwards.

When the swallow pose has been stabilized, he straightens his legs and turns to face corner 8. The method of returning the girl to the floor is the same as in previous examples.

In this lift, the boy places his right hand around the girl's waist if she lands on his right shoulder, but uses his left hand if her landing is on his left shoulder. The boy must do a full turn if she starts from point 7.

Jump to the Boy's Shoulder into Swallow Pose

The girl stands in the farthest corner of the stage at corner 6 and faces corner 2 on her right foot in pose croisée devant à terre. The boy is four to five steps away from her in a diagonal from corner 6 to 2, facing her. The girl runs and does petit assemblé right foot and, pressing strongly away from the floor, jumps towards the boy and assumes the swallow pose while in the air calculating her jump to land on his left shoulder with both thighs firmly held and still. At the moment when she jumps, the boy places his right hand with palm downward to hold the girl over her waist, then with a small bend of his knees, he brings his left shoulder forward and curves his left arm under her thighs. ONLY WHEN HE HAS CAUGHT HER, must he stretch his legs.

At a later time, as the boy brings his left arm forward, he may do a half-turn clockwise toward corner 2. The girl should practice moving from a run and pushing herself off the floor from pas sissonne from one foot.

During all the first attempts of his lift, the boy must begin by facing the girl. If she is fearful as she finishes, she should place her left hand over his left.

Saut De Basque onto the Boy's Chest

The preparation is the same as in the previous exercise. The girl, for this movement, must jump higher than before because she must aim for the boy's shoulder. During her jump, the boy must present his right shoulder and straighten carefully without displacing any of her weight. In this movement, the boy must catch the girl with both hands on her waist.

Jump to the Boy's Shoulder into Sitting Position

The girl stands with her back to corner 2 on her left foot, pose croisée devant à terre. The boy faces her from three to four steps away in an enlarged Fourth Position with his center of balance firmly over his left foot. The position must NOT be turned out. His right arm is stretched forward and his left is to the side. Both arms must be at shoulder level, palms up. The girl does pas couru on the right and strongly pressing the left to the floor, jumps onto the boy's right shoulder, her right hip pressed against the boy's neck. The girl's spine should be absolutely stretched and vertical, but slightly turned from the waist upward toward the boy's head. As the girl jumps into the sitting position, the boy must slightly bend his knees and, without pulling his right shoulder backward, offer it and catch the girl as she flies through the air. (Sketch 84a. Preparation for jump into sitting pose; 84b. Flight to sitting position; 84c. Final pose on boy's shoulder.)

The Ins and Outs of the Fish Pose when Resting on the Boy's Shoulder

1. Change into Fish from Sitting

As the girl sits on the boy's right shoulder, his left arm supports her right side and holds her waist between his finger and thumb, while his right hand on her right hip holds her upright as in the final pose of the previous exercise. The girl then stretches her right leg forward and, making a grand rond de jambe, takes the fish pose facing point 7. The change of support from shoulder to fish pose is

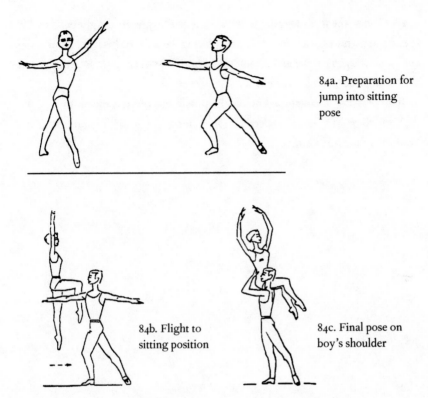

84a. Preparation for jump into sitting pose

84b. Flight to sitting position

84c. Final pose on boy's shoulder

not noticed by the audience when the change occurs with the boy's back to the audience. Changes when the girl is on the boy's shoulder may include turning a half or full circle in place.

2. Change from Fish to Swallow Pose on the Boy's Shoulder with a Turn

The girl is in fish facing point 3 in the boy's arms. With a slight bend of his knees, he throws her upwards, and turns her toward himself with both arms. At the moment of being thrown, the girl must energetically help the turn by swiftly raising her arms to Third and lifting her body upwards as she takes the swallow pose on the boy's left shoulder. She makes this movement the same way she would in fouetté en tournant, that is, swiftly straightening her right leg, which is bent at the knee, into Fifth Position and then simultaneously bending both legs at the knee in order to arrive in the swallow pose.

As soon as the girl's legs are straightened, the boy, with a slight bend of his knees, guides his left shoulder forward, placing the palm of his right hand at the middle of the girl's waist and his left under both hips as support. Resting her on his shoulder he turns to face corner 8.

If the teacher is concerned about the possibility of an accident during the study of these lifts, he or a spotter should stand facing the boy and place his hand under the girl's body.

12 · Aerial Overhead Lifts and Jumps

SEREBRENNIKOV begins this chapter with a warning: "Complicated lifts and throws are not necessarily studied by the entire class. The teacher must consider individual possibilities, including the boy's professional experience and his physical preparedness. The teacher must be careful to see that the boy's body is in the correct position at all times. In class, as a rule, the girl returns to the floor in a demi-plié to avoid harm to her ankles and knees."

Principle for Lifting from Shoulder to Overhead Poses

The principles for lifting the girl in the air with both hands either in place or with a run are as follows: The boy bends both knees in a deeper demi-plié and gives the first push by stretching his legs to the fullest extent. As he swiftly lifts the girl upwards, he again does a light demi-plié which is more like a bounce, and completes the lift on fully stretched legs. The greater part of the strain of lifting depends upon the strength and accurate movement of the boy's legs.

The girl must be centered exactly over the boy's head when she is finally fixed at the full length and height of his arms. In order to achieve this correctly, the moment she is lifted he must make a short step forwards as if to get below her body, but he must in no way bend at the waist as this may lead to spinal injury. The teacher must INSIST that the boy accomplish the lift with the correct placement of his body.

During lessons, after a lift, the girl generally should return to the floor in demi-plié.

Overhead Lift from Grand Jeté to First Arabesque

The girl stands in Fifth Position, her left foot devant, arms in Preparatory Position. The boy stands behind her near to her right shoulder, both hands on her waist. With a demi-plié and glissade starting with the right foot and without a change, the girl strongly presses from the floor with the left foot into grand jeté in First Arabesque towards point 3. SHE MUST JUMP UPWARDS ONLY AND NOT THROW HER BODY FORWARD. The boy, without leaving hold of her waist, and as she does glissade, lightly changes the line of his hands on her waist, the left slightly backwards towards and under her left shoulder blade, his right slightly forward. He must also direct the fingers of both hands upwards. (Sketch 85. Crest of the jump in grand jeté in First Arabesque.)

As the girl jumps, the boy swiftly moves to lift her overhead by stretching both arms upwards, not allowing himself to move forwards, so that he can softly lower the girl to the floor in fondu. As an alternative, he may allow himself one or two steps as he catches her, thus giving the audience the illusion of a longer flight. The shape of the movement in the grand jeté follows the natural trajectory of a smooth and even half-circle.

85. Crest of the jump in grand jeté in First Arabesque

Overhead Lift from Grand Jeté En Tournant En Attitude

The girl stands in attitude croisée à terre on her left foot. The boy is behind her in a lunge on the left foot, both hands on her waist. (Sketch 86a. Preparation for lift in grand jeté en tournant in attitude.) The girl does fondu into pas glissade, right foot, and pushes away from the floor with her left foot moving into grand jeté en tournant en attitude. The boy moves, simultaneously with the girl in pas

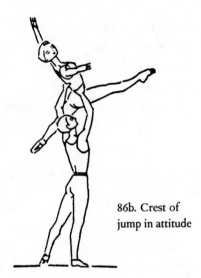

86a. Preparation for lift in grand
jeté en tournant in attitude

86b. Crest of
jump in attitude

glissade, a little distance from the girl and changes the line of his hands on her waist, the left slightly upwards toward her left shoulder blade and the right along her waist.

As the girl jumps, he swiftly stretches both arms, lifting and directing her toward corner 8. (Sketch 86b. Crest of the jump in attitude.) He then transfers the central weight of her body from the left to his right arm and lowers her softly to the floor on her right foot in fondu in attitude croisée. During the lift, the boy adheres to the basic principles for the placement of the palms of the hands. The girl MUST JUMP UPWARDS ONLY and without thrusting her body forward.

Overhead Lift in Grand Pas De Basque

The girl stands in Fifth Position, arms in Preparatory Position. The boy is behind her, both hands on her waist. The girl does pas glissade beginning with the right foot and without changing and coupé with the left foot into grand pas de basque turning toward corner 2. As she does pas glissade, the boy changes the line of his hands on her body so that the heels of his hands are pressed together while his fingers embrace the body. As the girl jumps, she allows her body to curve backward at the shoulders a little more than she would in solo work so that she receives support from the boy's arm.

At the moment the girl jumps, the boy, at the same time, draws her toward himself, carries her overhead in the direction of the jump towards corner 2, and lowers her to the floor softly in demi-plié.

Grand pas de chat is performed in the same way.

Overhead Lift from Jeté Entrelacé Face En Face

The girl stands with her back to point 7 on her left foot, pose croisée derrière à terre. The boy faces her about one step away in any pose suggested by the teacher. Beginning with her right foot, the girl steps and then moves into jeté élancé along a straight line from point 7 to 3, placing both hands firmly on both the boy's shoulders.

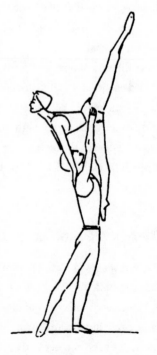

She must jump so that her hands are placed just over the top of his shoulders and the center of her weight exactly over the boy's central line of balance. During the jump, her head must be inclined slightly backward. (Sketch 87. Crest of the jump in jeté entrelacé with partners facing each other.)

The boy holds both hands on her body so that they are on top of her hips, but during the lift, he must change the position of his wrists very slightly so that his fingers move upwards a little to hold her waist very firmly.

As the girl jumps, the boy must take a small step forwards in order to get below her body as he lifts her above his head. He simultaneously turns toward point 3 as he steps, and lowers her softly to the floor in demi-plié.

87. Crest of jump in jeté entrelacé with partners facing each other

Aerial Tour by the Girl with Support by Both Hands on the Waist

The girl stands in Fifth Position, right foot devant. She does relevé sur les pointes, right arm in First Position, left arm in Second. From relevé, she descends into a strong demi-plié and pushes upwards making a full tour en l'air to the right at 360 degrees. During the tour, the girl's arms help the force of the turn by moving sharply into Third Position. The boy stands behind the girl with both hands on her waist. As she pushes upwards for the tour, he helps her gain height by throwing her upwards, and at the crest of the jump, he gives force to her tour in the direction of the turn.

After she completes the tour, he catches her at the waist and sets her carefully onto the floor. Or, as a more complicated ending, the girl may land on the boy's right shoulder in a sitting pose.

The girl must maintain her Fifth Position with her arms in Third Position throughout the movement. The partners may practice the tour en l'air, ending with the boy catching the girl with both arms around her thighs.

Lifts in a Fixed Position on Fully Stretched Arms

The girl stands in Fifth Position, right foot devant, arms in Preparatory Position. The boy is behind her, hands on her waist. The girl does demi-plié and jumps upwards raising her arms to Third. At the highest point, she bends her body backwards from waist and shoulder blades. As the girl jumps, the boy lifts her by slightly bending his knees when taking one step forward in order to get under her body. He simultaneously places his hands under her waist so that the heels of his palms are pressed together and the tips of the fingers of both hands hold her waist. (Sketch 88. Crest of the lift holding girl beneath her waist.)

88. Crest of the lift holding the girl beneath her waist

During the return to the floor, the girl must straighten her body as she slides down from the chest of the boy and finish in Fifth Position demi-plié.

Overhead Lift with Girl in First Arabesque in Place

In theater work, lifting the girl into the air is usually performed on the right side as a basic principle since the left side, because of the position of the heart, must not encounter too much strain or pressure. It is not usual to study the exercises on the left side nor to use the boy's left arm, because it is typically weaker than the right, even if the boy is left-handed.

The girl takes First Arabesque on pointe with the boy behind her, both hands on her body. When he feels that the girl is steady, he takes a half step forward on his right foot, bends his knees slightly, draws his right hand under her diaphragm (a little nearer the right side than the left), and places his left hand under her left thigh. His hands must be at the same level and the width of his shoulder apart, palms upward, fingers widely stretched, holding the girl equally on both right and left hands. (Sketch 89a. Preparation; Sketch 89b. Lift at the chest after the first demi-plié; Sketch 89c. Lift overhead after second slight demi-plié.)

It is vital that the girl hold her First Arabesque strongly at the moment when she is lifted from the floor. She must UNDER NO CIRCUMSTANCE incline her body forward nor bend the working left leg.

To lower the girl to the floor, the boy must allow her to reach his chest before bending his knees. At that moment, she stretches her right leg and, as her toe touches the floor, she must gradually sink into fondu in order to hold her own weight.

This lift should not frighten any girl as long as she maintains her pose. Anyone who is afraid should be helped by someone holding her left arm and another her right. The lift can also be studied at the beginning by lifting the girl only to the chest.

Overhead Lift in Third Arabesque

The girl stands with her back to point 7, the boy facing her three to four steps away in a straight line between point 7 to 3. The poses are given by the teacher. The girl runs and, without passing the boy, does sissonne tombée on her left foot, pushing strongly into and immediately from the floor, and jumps upwards in Third Arabesque toward point 3.

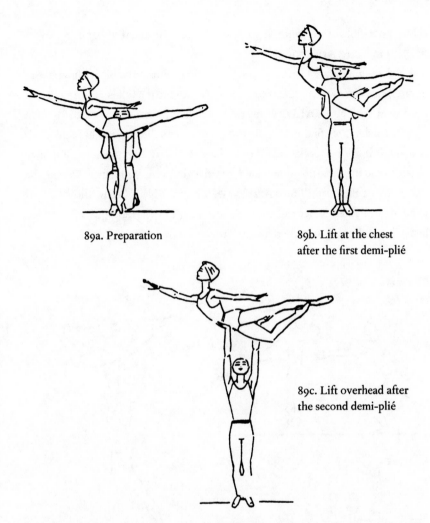

89a. Preparation

89b. Lift at the chest
after the first demi-plié

89c. Lift overhead after
the second demi-plié

It is important before the lift that the boy's hands are absolutely at the same level. The girl's right leg, when she jumps, must be fully straight and not above 100 degrees from the floor (higher would make it difficult to catch and hold the pose in the air). She must jump as if to go above the boy but not fly over him. The palm of his right hand must be placed so that his fingers point slightly upward. The left hand is also opened palm up, but his fingers are stretched downward. As the girl does sissonne tombée, he must stretch both arms forwards and, lunging onto his left leg, place his right hand on her hip and his left hand about the middle of her right thigh. (Sketch 90a. Placement of hands for over-head lift in Third Arabesque.)

He then immediately steps forwards and lifts her as he stabilizes her pose in Third Arabesque with his arms stretched overhead to the fullest. During the lift the boy MUST NOT ALLOW his right shoulder to move backwards.

The teacher may find it necessary to stand behind the boy and hold the girl's two hands if the boy collapses. Should the girl misjudge her distance, a spotter or teacher in the same position would give the girl more confidence. During the first study of this lift in Third Arabesque, it is advisable NOT to allow the girl to bend her left leg to her right as in Sketch 90b (Third Arabesque with left leg bent), but to leave it stretched downward.

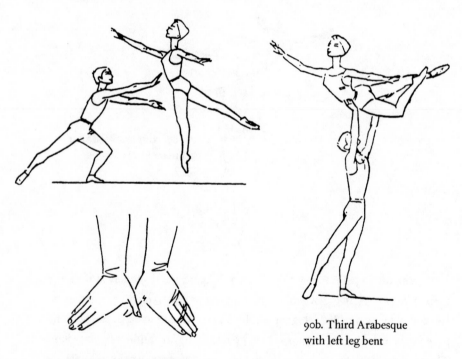

90b. Third Arabesque
with left leg bent

90a. Placement of hands for
overhead lift in Third Arabesque

Overhead Lift in Fourth Arabesque with Grand Fouetté Sauté

This lift in Fourth Arabesque should first be executed without a jump and using the same principles as those for lifting the girl in First Arabesque.

The girl stands in First Arabesque facing corner 2. The boy stands two steps behind her on a diagonal between corners 2 to 6 in the same or another pose given by the teacher. The girl does pas glissade towards the boy, then strongly pushes the left foot from the floor into grand fouetté, ending in Fourth Arabesque. She must jump UPWARDS and fly over her partner but NOT PAST HIM. The Fourth Arabesque pose in the air must be absolutely correct and will depend entirely on her control over her body and its direction. The boy catches and lifts her at that moment when her jump in grand fouetté has turned into Fourth Arabesque. His right hand must find the girl's right side and his left the center of her right thigh. (Sketch 91. Crest of the lift in Fourth Arabesque.) When lowering the girl to the floor, the boy bends his elbows and lowers her to chest level. Only then does he bend his knees to allow her to sink to the floor in Fourth Arabesque fondue.

If the teacher is afraid that the lift will not succeed, he or a spotter should stand about one step away facing the boy and hold the girl's torso with his left hand.

The preparatory jump in most lifts is more like a grand temps levé or sissonne in Fourth Arabesque, because at the moment of flight, the girl must be in Fourth Arabesque and MUST NOT TURN IN THE BOY'S ARMS WHILE PERFORMING A GRAND FOUETTÉ. SHOULD SHE DO SO, SHE WILL SLIP THROUGH HIS ARMS.

91. Crest of the lift in Fourth Arabesque

Lift Overhead in Swallow Pose from a Run

The girl stands back to point 7 on her right foot, pose croisée devant à terre. The boy faces her, back to point 3, from five to six steps away along a straight line between points 7 to 3. The girl does pas couru towards the boy and, without passing him, falls into pas tombé on her left foot, strongly presses from the floor, and is lifted into swallow pose. As the girl jumps, both her hips must be on an exact level with the boy's shoulders. She must calculate her run and jump so that she does not fly past him, but jumps as if to go over him. As the girl does sissonne tombée, the boy bends his knees slightly and places both hands on her hips so that the strain of holding her weight firmly rests on the heels of the palms of his hands. His fingers must rest on the front of the girl's lower ribs. As she jumps, he lifts her and stabilizes her swallow pose at the fullest stretch of his arms. (Sketch 92. Crest of the lift in swallow pose.)

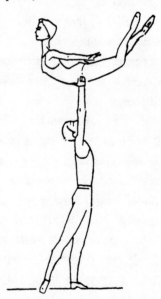

When the girl finishes a pose with her body held in a finely stretched curve from the head to the toes, she must NEVER allow her spine or head to drop forward OR THERE WILL BE AN ACCIDENT.

The best way to lower the girl to the floor from this lift is to have the boy bend his elbows and lower the girl to his chest level. At the same time, the girl stretches her right leg downward, and he bends his knees to place her softly on the floor in fondu or demi-plié.

If the teacher is afraid that the lift will not succeed, he must stand about one step away from the boy's back and, should there be a mishap, catch the girl by her arms or her shoulders.

92. Crest of the lift in swallow pose

When the girl studies the swallow pose using fully stretched legs and curving her body backward as an exercise in her classes, she must not consider it an acrobatic feat, but a small part of the repertoire of a classical dancer.

Overhead Lift in Saut De Basque Ending in the Sitting Position

The girl stands facing corner 2 on her left foot in Second Arabesque à terre. The boy is behind her three to four steps away in the same pose. The girl does pas chassé towards the boy and does saut de basque with such accuracy that the jump finishes on a level with his chest in the sitting position. Serebrennikov insists that the girl must learn to jump to this level.

As the girl does her saut de basque, the boy bends his knees slightly and takes a step backwards onto his right foot, places his hands on her buttocks at the "sit" bones and lifts her, stabilizing her sitting position on fully stretched arms. (Sketch 93. Crest of sitting pose on the partner's fully stretched arms.)

Again, it is essential to lift the girl to chest level. Only then, when this position is assured, must the boy practice stretching his arms to their fullest. To lower the girl to the floor, the boy follows the instructions in the previous exercises.

If the teacher fears that the lift will fail, he or a spotter must stand behind the boy about one step away and, in case of misjudgment, catch the girl with two hands on her waist.

93. Crest of sitting pose on the partner's fully stretched arms

Overhead Lift in First Arabesque from Grand Jeté

The girl does pas glissade beginning with the right foot and pushes strongly from the floor with the left into grand jeté in First Arabesque toward point 3. The boy lifts her sharply with his right hand and quickly places his left hand beneath her left hip, thereby stabilizing her position in First Arabesque at the highest possible stretch of his arms.

To achieve the full height of this lift, the girl must transfer her weight slightly forward on the boy's right arm so that his left hand has a brief moment to change its position to under her left thigh.

If the teacher is afraid that this lift will be imprecisely timed, he or a spotter should face the direction of the lift and place the left hand under the girl's torso and move simultaneously with the lift and brief transfer of weight.

Other examples should be studied with the girl using grand jeté en attitude effacée.

13 · Aerial Overhead Lifts with One-hand Support

THE AERIAL LIFTS and throws in the last few chapters are suitable for the theatrical category of ballroom dance as well as for nightclub and exhibition performances. Provided the girl's heels are not too high nor the costume too voluminous, all the movements that are not en pointe should be studied with the same care—including the added security of a spotter's presence—as that taken when working in the classical repertoire.

Overhead Lifts in Fixed Poses with One-hand Support

Serebrennikov tells us that without exception, all the lifts in fixed poses on one hand take place with the active participation of the boy's other hand. The positions are explained in each exercise. The study of these exercises must only proceed when the students are able to coordinate their movements with their partners.

Lifting with the Girl Held under Her Waist

The girl stands in Fifth Position sur les pointes, right foot devant, arms in arabesque. The boy is behind her, in a near-kneeling position on his right knee, hands on her waist. The girl bends her left knee (not too turned-out), the toe resting just behind her right calf. The boy places his right hand on the center of her body, his first finger and thumb stretched open along the waist line, palm fully flattened against her pelvis. His left hand is placed just below the girl's left knee. (Sketch 94a. Preparation for lift under the girl's waist.) The girl does fondu and jumps upwards, strongly pushing away from the floor with the right foot. At that moment, the boy gives her a slight signal and lifts her WITH BOTH ARMS and when his right arm is fully stretched at the elbow, the girl smoothly bends backwards from her waist and shoulder girdle. (Sketch 94b. Crest of the lift with one hand at the waist.) This allows the boy to balance and support her with one hand. The boy then stretches his left arm into Second, and the girl remains firmly stabilized on his right arm. She then stretches her left leg downward to join the right in Fifth Position. THE GIRL'S LEFT LEG, BENT AT THE KNEE, MUST BE HELD ABSOLUTELY STEADY, FIRM, AND STILL DURING THE LIFT, IN ORDER TO ALLOW THE BOY TO USE BOTH ARMS.

The best way to lower the girl to the floor is for the boy to place his left hand around and toward the left side of the girl's waist as she smoothly straightens her body. Once he has the girl in both arms, he lowers her softly to the floor in demi-plié.

The artistic quality of this lift depends entirely upon its smoothness. Throughout, the boy must keep his right hand firmly fixed on the girl's waist and his left just below her left knee. As she jumps, she must strongly stretch her

94b. Crest of the lift with one hand at the waist

94a. Preparation for lift with one hand at the waist

left leg downward as if she wants to step on it. In this way, she definitely helps her partner and makes the lift look and feel lighter.

Lift with the Girl in Sitting Position

The preparation is the same as in the preceding exercise. The boy then bends his knees deeply and places his left hand just below the girl's left knee and the palm of his right hand under her buttocks. The girl, sur les pointes, does fondu and pushes herself strongly from the floor to jump upwards. At this moment, the boy lifts her with both arms and then lets go with his left hand to hold the girl firmly on the right hand in the sitting position. During the lift, the girl must hold her body absolutely still from the waist upward, shoulders held down and the pelvic muscles drawn together. SHE MUST NEVER, IN ANY OF THESE LIFTS, LOOK DOWN, BECAUSE THE DISPLACEMENT OF HER HEAD WILL DISTURB THE BALANCE OF THE LIFT AND MAY CAUSE AN INJURY TO HERSELF AND HER PARTNER. A glance in the mirror to check her position should be sufficient. She must learn to feel her positions and to trust her partner, especially with a spotter present. (Sketch 95. Three poses sitting on the partner's right hand.)

95. Three poses sitting on the partner's right hand

To lower the girl to the floor, the boy takes the girl's left knee in his left hand and lowers her to chest level, then bends deeply to place her on the floor on one foot.

The girl, when in the sitting position on the boy's hand, straightens her left leg, bringing it into the air in Fifth Position. The boy then places his left hand on her diaphragm and lowers her to the floor on two feet.

Alternatively, the boy may lower the girl onto his chest, where she changes into fish facing point 7. He then places his left arm below her waist and holds her right thigh upwards with his right hand. This lift can also be performed by throwing the girl into the air during the change of pose.

Lift with Saut De Basque Ending by Sitting on the Boy's Hand

The girl stands facing corner 8 on her left foot, the right pointe tendue derrière on a diagonal toward corner 4, her right arm in Third Position and her left in Second. The boy is behind her about three to four steps away along the same diagonal and the same pose. The girl does a short pas chassé with her right and a saut de basque making a three-quarter turn in the air and calculating to rise to the height of the boy's chest in a sitting position. In this case, her left side will descend onto his chest. As the girl does pas chassé, the boy must deeply bend both knees and, when she turns her left side toward him, catch her with his right hand under her buttocks, his left hand under her left knee.

The girl's jump lightens the weight of the lift, and the pose must be absolutely stabilized when the boy releases his left hand.

The return to the floor is the same as in the preceding examples.

Grand Jeté with Lift on Boy's Arm

The girl stands with her back to corner 4 on her left foot in pose croisée devant à terre. The boy is behind her and by her left shoulder, right hand on her right side near the bottom of her right shoulder blade. He holds the girl's left hand in his left, palm to palm. His feet are in the same position as the girl's.

The girl does glissade followed by grand jeté en attitude effacée on a diagonal toward corner 8. (Sketch 96a. Jeté in attitude effacée.) The boy does glissade with her, leading her with his left hand, elbow bent and held near her left hip. As the girl jumps, he lifts her with BOTH HANDS. She pushes herself upwards by pressing her left hand on his left, but without raising her shoulders.

She must arch her back as well as her shoulder girdle strongly. Only the boy's right arm takes the weight of the girl's body and, when it is stabilized, he immediately opens his left arm to the side. (Sketch 96b. Final pose with one hand on waist.) When first studying this lift, the boy should not release the girl's hand and NEVER push her arm upwards. THE GIRL MUST PUSH HERSELF.

The girl's return to the floor can be accomplished by the boy's taking her left hand and bringing it toward her hip. Without straightening her body, the girl joins her feet in Fifth Position. The boy, bending his knees, places both arms around the girl and, as she straightens, lowers her to the floor in demi-plié.

In another return, the boy places his left hand on the girl's diaphragm; when she finishes her jump, she can then move into attitude or stretch to First or Second Arabesque.

If the teacher is concerned that the lift will be badly timed, he or a spotter should stand behind the boy and, if necessary, place his hands under the girl's back.

96a. Jeté in attitude effacée

96b. Final pose with one hand on waist

Throws into the Air with and without Change of Pose

Before throwing the girl into the air from a stabilized pose on fully stretched arms, the boy must make a quick plié, keeping his body absolutely straight, his arms or arm fully stretched, and then quickly stretch his knees just after he has caught the girl.

Throwing the Girl from First Arabesque to Fish

The girl is held in the air in First Arabesque in the boy's arms, facing point 3. The boy bends his knees slightly and throws the girl straight upwards and then catches her in fish pose with his right arm under her body and his left over her left thigh.

In this lift, the girl must move accurately as she changes and must in no way stiffen. The boy cushions her change by stretching his legs. His body must remain absolutely straight.

If the teacher fears that the lift will be inaccurately timed, he or a spotter should stand facing the boy and place the left hand under the girl's torso.

Throwing from First Arabesque into Fish with a Turn of the Body

This lift is executed from First Arabesque as above (in the air). The boy throws the girl slightly upwards as she immediately joins her legs together in Fifth Position, raising her arms in Third while turning to bring the right shoulder to the front, and moving into the fish pose facing point 7. The boy places his left arm under her body and his right over her right thigh. In moving from one pose to the other, the girl must not sit on the boy's chest. Her hip must at all times be strongly directed forward, her body held strongly at the waist and shoulder girdle, her head stretched up and backwards.

Throwing from Fourth Arabesque into Fish with a Small Air Turn

Both partners begin facing corner 8 in Fourth Arabesque. The boy throws the girl up lightly. At the same time, the girl must stretch her legs into Fifth Position momentarily, raise her arms to Third just turning her body to the left, and assume the fish pose facing point 3. In this case, the boy must throw the girl upwards more strongly, but catch her in the same way as above.

Throwing the Girl from Swallow to Fish with a Full Turn

The girl is in swallow on the boy's left shoulder as in a previous exercise (jeté entrelacé to the boy's shoulder). The boy lightly tosses the girl straight upwards. At that moment, she makes a full turn to the right, moving into the horizontal position, joining her feet in Fifth and strongly raising her arms to Third. After the turn, she takes the fish pose facing point 3. The boy catches her with his right arm under her body and places his left hand over her thigh.

Double Tour En L'air in Horizontal Position

This exercise uses three jumps: jeté entrelacé; assemblé en tournant; and horizontal turns en l'air taken with extreme force.

The girl is in a high First Arabesque on her right pointe. The boy is three to four steps away from her in a straight line between points 3 and 7, in the same pose à terre. The girl does pas chassé towards the boy, tombé on left foot, and with a brush right towards point 7 rises in the air into the horizontal position. She quickly joins her left foot to her right and raises her arms to Third. She must judge her preparation and jump so that her hips are in front of the boy's chest and so that she takes force for the turn at the highest point of her flight. The boy places both hands on her waist and throws her strongly upwards as he gives impetus for the turn to her left side toward himself. His right hand is slightly above her waist and toward her right shoulder blade. This helps to keep the girl in the horizontal position. His left hand reaches above her body toward her right hip, because he must actively throw her upwards and give impetus to her turn with his hand.

After a double turn in the air in the horizontal position, the girl goes into the fish pose as the boy catches her body with his right hand and her left thigh with his left hand. (Sketch 97. Position of the girl in horizontal turns overhead.)

This lift demands absolute coordination of movement and common tempo from both boy and girl. Therefore it requires more practice than any other lift.

With it, we are at the end of our textbook for the study of beautiful pas de deux dance. There are many more lifts to be discovered by professional dancers. The following sketches show a few of them. Note the expressiveness of the poses, the flexible and strong upper back of the female dancers, and the clear stability presented by the male dancers. All these things, plus a strong aesthetic sense, comprise the beauty of pas de deux dance.

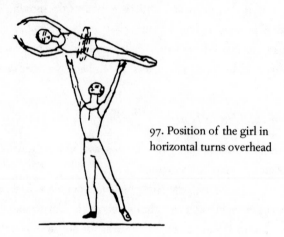

97. Position of the girl in horizontal turns overhead

Arabesque in nineteenth-century ballet. Zh. Ayupova and A. Lunev in *Giselle*.

First Arabesque facing partner. N. Arkhipova and L. Nikonov in *Classic Pas de Deux*.

Fourth Arabesque with cradle support. I. Kolpakova and V. Semyonov in *Romeo and Juliet*.

First Arabesque penchée. I. Kolpakova and V. Semyonov in *Sleeping Beauty*.

Attitude croisée with one-hand support. T. Terekhova and K. Zaklinsky in *La Bayadère*.

Off-balance First Arabesque. T. Terekhova and K. Zaklinsky in *La Bayadère*.

First Arabesque with one-hand support. E. Yevteyeva and A. Bosov in *Butterfly*.

First Arabesque with one-hand support at back of waist. A. Osipenko and D. Markovsky in *Swan Lake*.

Fall to the side. G. Mezentaeva and S. Berezhnoy in *Swan Lake*.

Fall backwards with shoulder support. E. Yevteyeva and G. Babanin in *La Bayadère*.

Attitude effacée with fall backwards and shoulder support. I. Kolpakova and A. Gribov in *Legend of Love*.

Attitude croisée on partner's thigh with one-hand waist support. G. Mezentseva and S. Berezhnoy in *Swan Lake*.

Second Arabesque on partner's thigh with knee support. O. Likhovskaya and A. Bosov in *Conception*.

Fall onto partner's knees, arms holding waist for support. O. Likhovskaya and A. Bosov in *Conception*.

Girl supporting herself on partner's lower legs. I. Kolpakova and S. Berezhnoy in *Romeo and Juliet*.

Knee support in contemporary ballet. I. Kolpakova and U. Solovyov in *The Two*.

First Arabesque with shoulder support. O. Likhovskaya and A. Bosov in *Conception*.

Fifth Position with chest support and arm cradling partner's back. A. Osipenko and D. Markovsky in *Antony and Cleopatra*.

Chest and one-arm cradle support. Ch. Babaeva and V. Pletnev in *Seven Beauties*.

Lift with two-hand support on pelvis. E. Yevteyeva and A. Bosov in *Butterfly*.

Shoulder and knee support. N. Bolshakova and V. Gulyaev in *Creation of the World*.

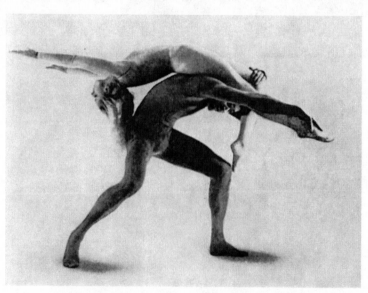

Lean from sit on shoulder. A. Osipenko and D. Markovsky in *Minotaur and a Nymph*.

Fifth Position with thigh support. E. Yevteyeva and G. Babanin in *La Bayadère*.

Shoulder lift with partners facing opposite directions. I. Zubkovskaya and S. Kuznetsov in *Legend of Love*.

Lift with shoulder and hip support. E. Yevteyeva and G. Babanin in *La Bayadère*.

Fall to the side with legs raised and cradle support around waist. S. Yefremova and A. Bosov in a concert piece.

Toss from chest lift. G. Kekisheva and A. Pavlovsky in *Laurencia*.

Crest of the jump in grand jeté in First Arabesque. E. Yevteyeva and A. Bosov in *Butterfly*.

First Arabesque with both partners in sauté. N. Bolshakova and V. Gulyaev in *Chopiniana*.

Ending in attitude croisée after grand fouetté sauté with support by one hand. N. Sveshnikova and F. Razumatov in *Chopiniana*.

Crest of lift, partner held beneath her waist. T. Terekhova and K. Zaklinsky in *La Bayadère*.

Overhead sit lift with partner's support on buttocks. O. Kikhovskaya and A. Bosov in *Conception*.

Two-hand overhead lift with support on hips and shoulders. A. Osipenko and A. Gribov in *Stone Flower*.

Overhead lift with support at waist and thigh. T. Terekhova and K. Zaklinsky in *La Bayadère*.

Fifth Position lift with support on thighs. A. Osipenko and D. Markovsky in *Talioni's Flight*.

Overhead one-hand support at back of waist. N. Bolshakova and V. Gulyaev in *Walpurghis Nacht*.

Overhead First Arabesque with one-hand support on hip. G. Komleva and B. Budarin in *Don Quixote*.

Toss in First Arabesque. S. Yefremova and A. Bosov in a concert piece.

First Arabesques in jeté sauté as exit. T. Terekhova and K. Zaklinsky in *La Bayadère*.

Nikolai Serebrennikov was an artist of the Kirov Ballet. He first wrote this book in 1969 when he was teaching advanced partnering techniques at the Leningrad (St. Petersburg) Choreographic Institute. He is now the Dance Master at the Vaganova Ballet Academy.

Marian Horosko is the former education editor of *Dance Magazine*. She was a member of the New York City Ballet and the Metropolitan Opera Ballet, and performed on Broadway in *Oklahoma!* and in the film *An American in Paris*. She is the author of two other textbooks on dance.

CPSIA information can be obtained at www.ICGtesting.com
Printed in the USA
LVOW062252261112

308883LV00003B/986/P